# The Ultimate Classi

## CONTE_

| | |
|---|---|
| Page 2: | Introduction |
| Page 3: | About the book |

*Part One: The Questions*

Pages 4 to 63

*Part Two: The Answers*

Pages 64 to 78:

*Part Three: The Stories*

Pages 79 to 227: The stories behind the answers

Pages 228: About the authors

# Introduction

Having waited, er, quite a few years to write a book, I've now written two in a few months. Which just goes to show that ~~there's no fool like an old fool~~ it's all about overcoming inertia and getting on with what you really want to do.

When I started writing *The Ultimate Unofficial F1 Quiz Book* (try saying that after a couple of drams), I decided that I wanted to share my royalties (assuming there were any...) with charity.

That's something I plan to stick with, so at least 25% of my royalties from this and any subsequent books I write will go to charity.

Details of the charities that have benefited will be posted from time to time on my website: www.thelosthighway.online.

In the meantime, please accept my thanks for purchasing this book. I hope that you enjoy it.

Finally, a word or two about copyright.

All trademarks mentioned within the pages of this book are the property of their respective owners.

In all other regards, copyright in the text of this book is held by me, David Milloy, as is copyright in the rear cover photo. Copyright in and to the front cover illustration is held by Marcus T. Ward.

# About this book

It seems appropriate to start with a question, so here's one to ponder: 'When is a quiz book not a quiz book?'

When it's a history book as well.

To explain: there are fifteen multiple choice sections, each containing ten questions.

So far, so quiz book.

But where this book differs from other quiz books is that for every multiple-choice question there's a story that contains facts, statistics and/or trivia that relates to the question, the answer to it, or both. It's therefore a history book (of sorts) as well as a quiz book.

Facts are facts, and this book is full of them. I hope – and believe – that they are all accurate. Any errors are down to me.

As for opinions, well, we've all got them. Unless otherwise attributed, the ones in this book are, for better or worse, mine and mine alone.

It's not the easiest quiz you'll ever have a crack at, but hopefully it'll be one of the most enjoyable and informative. That's the idea, anyway!

Have fun.

David M. Milloy
November, 2020

# General Knowledge 1

**G1**

Edsel was a short-lived brand owned by which company?

A.  General Motors

B.  Ford

C.  Chrysler

D.  Studebaker

**G2**

In the 1985 film *A View to a Kill*, what car does James Bond commandeer in Paris?

A.  Renault 11

B.  Citroën 2CV

C.  Citroën BX

D.  Renault 20

**G3**

When introduced in 1960, the UK MOT test applied to vehicles of what minimum age (in years)?

A.  7

B.  10

C.  3

D.  5

## G4

The BAT 5, BAT 7 and BAT 9 concept cars of the 1950s were all based on which chassis?

A. Buick Skylark

B. BMW 507

C. Alfa Romeo 1900

D. Dodge Royal

## G5

Which European car was advertised in the USA with the slogan "Think Small"?

A. VW Beetle

B. Austin Mini

C. Renault Le Car

D. Fiat 500

## G6

What was the name of the Michelotti-designed saloon built by Leyland Australia but never sold in the UK?

A. P40

B. P82

C. P37

D. P76

### G7

What was the first car to be used as a Safety Car in an F1 Grand Prix?

A. Porsche 914

B. Lamborghini Espada

C. Jensen Interceptor

D. BMW 3.0 CSL

### G8

In what year did the Citroën 2CV go into production?

A. 1953

B. 1946

C. 1949

D. 1950

### G9

The Saab 600 of the early 1980s was a rebadged...?

A. VW Golf

B. Ford Escort

C. Lancia Delta

D. Opel Astra

## G10

Which of the following Triumph cars has front-wheel drive?

A. Dolomite

B. 1300/1500

C. Toledo

D. 2000

## Film & TV

### F1

In which 1985 film did a Peugeot 205 GTI feature in a car chase?

A. Back to the Future

B. The Jewel of the Nile

C. Target

D. Police Story

### F2

The 'Turbo Interceptor' in the 1986 film 'The Wraith' was based on which concept car?

A. Dodge M4S

B. Aston Martin Bulldog

C. Ford Maya

D. Buick Questor

### F3

In the 1984 British film *'Comfort and Joy'*, what car does the main character, Alan 'Dickie' Bird, drive?

A. Ford Escort XR3i Cabriolet

B. Alfa Romeo Spider

C. BMW 323i Baur Cabriolet

D. VW Golf GLi Convertible

## F4

In the 1974 film '*The Longest Yard*', what car does Burt Reynolds dump in the river?

A. Fiat Dino Spider

B. Jaguar E-Type

C. De Tomaso Pantera

D. Citroën SM

## F5

Luke Skywalker's landspeeder in the film '*Star Wars*' was based on the chassis of which car?

A. Bond Bug

B. Fiat 126

C. Austin Mini

D. Peugeot 104

## F6

The futuristic car driven by Ed Straker in the 1970 TV series '*UFO*' was based on the chassis of which car?

A. Austin 1800

B. Ford Zodiac

C. Jaguar Mark 2

D. Rover 2000

## F7

In the 1969 film '*The Italian Job*', what car falls off a car transporter onto a parked police car?

A. Austin A60 Cambridge

B. Alfa Romeo Giulia

C. Renault 8

D. Fiat 124

## F8

In the 1985 film '*Back to the Future*', what speed does Doc Brown's modified De Lorean have to reach in order to achieve time travel?

A. 100 miles per hour

B. 56 miles per hour

C. 88 miles per hour

D. 72 miles per hour

## F9

What car does Gareth Cheeseman drive in the Steve Coogan comedy '*Dearth of a Salesman*'?

A. Ford Cougar

B. Vauxhall Calibra

C. Ford Probe

D. Rover 200 coupé

## F10

What model of Aston Martin does Lord Brett Sinclair drive in the TV series '*The Persuaders'?*

A. V8

B. DB6

C. DB5

D. DBS

# General Knowledge II

## G11

What was the UK's best-selling car of the 1980s?

A. Vauxhall Cavalier

B. Ford Escort

C. Ford Fiesta

D. Ford Sierra

## G12

What feature did the Volvo 343 have as standard when launched in 1976?

A. Anti-lock brakes

B. Continuously Variable Transmission

C. Four-wheel drive

D. Remote central locking

## G13

In which year was a four-cylinder version of the Rover SD1 first offered for sale in the UK?

A. 1980

B. 1978

C. 1982

D. There was no four-cylinder version

**G14**

Which manufacturer had an illuminated advertisement on the Eiffel Tower from 1925 to 1934?

A. Renault

B. Citroën

C. Peugeot

D. Simca

**G15**

Which company built the gas turbine engines that powered the prototype Advanced Passenger Train (APT-E) of the early 1970s?

A. Jaguar

B. Rover

C. Ford

D. Rolls-Royce

**G16**

The first-generation VW Polo was beaten into production by which near-identical Audi model?

A. Audi 60

B. Audi 70

C. Audi 40

D. Audi 50

## G17

Which one of the following Japanese cars **was** officially imported into the UK?

A.  Suzuki Cappuccino

B.  Nissan Figaro

C.  Honda Beat

D.  Autozam AZ-1

## G18

What was the name of the electric car built by Scottish Aviation Limited that appeared on the *'Tomorrow's World'* TV show in 1966?

A.  Scamp

B.  Atom

C.  Rascal

D.  Gnome

## G19

Which of the following hatchbacks went into production first?

A.  Simca 1100

B.  Renault 16

C.  Fiat 127

D.  Austin Maxi

## G20

What do the Maserati Khamsin, VW Passat, Pagani Zonda and Austin Maestro have in common?

A.  They did not meet US regulations and could not be sold there

B.  They were each the first car in their class to come with run-flat tyres

C.  They were all designed in Italy

D.  They share their name with a wind

## It's a Numbers Game I

### N1

In 1994, there were 27,500 Renault 18s licensed with the DVLA. How many were licensed as of the 2$^{nd}$ quarter of 2020?

A.  66

B.  17

C.  38

D.  23

### N2

How many Amphicars were built in its four year production run?

A.  1535

B.  3878

C.  5114

D.  2433

### N3

When were the Type Approval Regulations introduced to the UK?

A.  1975

B.  1973

C.  1972

D.  1977

## N4

How many examples of the first-generation Renault Espace were sold in its first month on sale?

A.  9

B.  43

C.  4

D.  21

## N5

How many Morris Marinas were sold in the UK in its most successful year?

A.  130,633

B.  95,158

C.  115,041

D.  80,714

## N6

What is the engine capacity of the Bugatti EB110 supercar?

A.  4600cc

B.  5100cc

C.  3500cc

D.  4000cc

## N7

In what year did Chrysler sell their European car manufacturing operation to PSA (Peugeot Société Anonyme)?

A.   1978

B.   1981

C.   1979

D.   1980

## N8

In what year did Alfa Romeo's celebrated V6 *Busso* engine first appear in a production car?

A.   1982

B.   1985

C.   1979

D.   1981

## N9

In which year did the Ford Fiesta first outsell the Mini in the UK?

A.   1977

B.   1980

C.   1979

D.   1981

**N10**

How long, to the nearest centimetre, was the 1981 Lincoln Town Car?

A.  602

B.  532

C.  557

D.  508

## General Knowledge III

### G21

Which sports car manufacturer also produced an all-wheel drive pick-up in the 1980s?

A. Ferrari

B. Porsche

C. Lamborghini

D. Maserati

### G22

The Hillman Hunter was built in Iran until 2005 under what name?

A. Pars

B. Samand

C. Paykan

D. Sarir

### G23

What was the first Japanese car to be officially imported to the UK?

A. Daihatsu Compagno

B. Subaru 360

C. Mazda Cosmo

D. Toyota 1000

**G24**

Which company manufactured Rostyle wheels in the UK?

A. GKN

B. Wolfrace

C. Rubery Owen

D. Minilite

**G25**

Which Mitsubishi-owned Australian marque sold a badge-engineered Mitsubishi Galant in the UK between 1982 and 1984?

A. Holden

B. Finch

C. Denning

D. Lonsdale

**G26**

The 'MR' in the name of the Toyota MR2 is an abbreviation of…?

A. Mid-engine, Rear-wheel drive

B. Masahiro Ryusaki

C. Midship Runabout

D. Maximum Responsiveness

## G27

Ferrari and Dodge each produced a model with which name?

A. Daytona

B. GTO

C. America

D. California

## G28

How many cars did Lotus build in 1981?

A. 762

B. 345

C. 509

D. 1,023

## G29

Which production car of the late 1980s and early 1990s had retractable doors?

A. Panther Solo 2

B. BMW Z1

C. Toyota Sera

D. Treser TR-1

**G30**

From what did the Matra M530 take its name?

A. A guided missile

B. The road that passed Matra's HQ

C. Its range in kilometres on a full tank of fuel

D. The number of people then employed by Matra Sports

## Motorsport

### M1

In which car did Andrew Cowan win the 1968 London-Sydney Marathon?

A. Hillman Hunter

B. Austin 1800

C. Ford Cortina GT

D. Rover 2000 TC

### M2

Which future F1 world champion raced in a round of the Volkswagen-organised Scirocco Junior Cup in 1976?

A. Nigel Mansell

B. Alain Prost

C. Keke Rosberg

D. Alan Jones

### M3

Where did the Renault 12 win a round of the World Rally Championship?

A. USA

B. France (Corsica)

C. Finland

D. Greece

## M4

Finland's Pauli Toivonen controversially won the 1966 Monte Carlo Rally in which car?

A.  Porsche 911T

B.  Saab 96

C.  Citroën DS 21

D.  Lancia Flavia

## M5

In 1980 and 1981, which car did Stirling Moss drive in the British Saloon Car Championship?

A.  Mazda RX-7

B.  Audi 80 GLE

**C.**  Ford Capri 3.0S

D.  Rover 3500 S

## M6

Bernard Unett won the British Saloon Car Championship three times at the wheel of which car?

A.  Hillman/Chrysler Avenger

B.  Mini 1275 GT

C.  Triumph Dolomite Sprint

D.  Toyota Celica GT

## M7

A Group B version of which of these cars was produced?

A. VW Golf

B. Citroën BX

C. BMW 3 Series

D. Lotus Esprit

## M8

The last two-wheel drive car to win the World Rally Championship was the...?

A. Ford Escort

B. Toyota Corolla

C. Lancia 037

D. Talbot Sunbeam Lotus

## M9

Which of these cars did **not** win the World Rally Constructors' Championship?

A. Talbot Sunbeam Lotus

B. Opel Ascona 400

C. Fiat 131 Abarth

D. Ford Escort RS1800

**M10**

In which car did Paul Newman win the first of his four SCCA championships?

A. Triumph TR6

B. Porsche 912

C. Lotus Elan

D. VW Rabbit (Golf)

## General Knowledge IV

### G31

What was the first water-cooled Volkswagen production car?

A.  Scirocco

B.  412

C.  Polo

D.  K70

### G32

What was unusual about the Rover T4 prototype of 1961?

A.  It was mid-engined

B.  It had a gas turbine engine

C.  It was electrically powered

D.  It was able to park itself

### G33

The Renault 7, a booted version of the Renault 5 hatchback, was built and (mostly) sold in which country?

A.  France

B.  Spain

C.  Romania

D.  Italy

### G34

What was the name of the coupé produced by Saab in the 1960s and 1970s?

A. Draken

B. Vihara

C. Vixen

D. Sonett

### G35

Which of the following cars did **not** use the same exterior door handles as the Morris Marina?

A. Morris Ital

B. Lotus Esprit

C. Austin Allegro

D. Reliant Scimitar SE6

### G36

In 1970, the members of England's squad for the 1970 football World Cup were each given the loan of which car?

A. Ford Cortina 1600E

B. Hillman Hunter GT

C. Ford Escort Sport

D. MGB GT

## G37

The Peugeot 309 was originally intended to be sold as the Talbot...?

A. Colorado

B. Arizona

C. Nevada

D. Montana

## G38

What was the first European production car to have a turbocharged engine?

A. Saab 99 Turbo

B. Porsche 930

C. BMW 2002 Turbo

D. Renault 18 Turbo

## G39

Which 1960s microcar was manufactured on the Isle of Man?

A. Peel P50

B. Colliday Chariot

C. Fairthorpe Atom

D. Scootacar

## G40

In what car did Lord Lucan flee from the scene of his alleged crimes in 1974?

A. Jaguar Mark 2

B. Triumph 2000

C. Mercedes 280CE

D. Ford Corsair

# It Pays To Advertise

### A1

What car was advertised on UK television with the slogan "Not the car for Mr. Average"?

A. Princess 2

B. Ford Cortina

C. Audi 80

D. Renault Fuego Turbo

### A2

Which car was promoted in the UK with the slogan "Built like Rocky"?

A. Matra Rancho

B. Citroën AX GT

C. Saab 900

D. Volvo 345

### A3

Which car was advertised as "The car you always promised yourself"?

A. Triumph TR7

B. Lancia Beta

C. Ford Capri

D. Opel Manta GT/E

## A4

The Ford Puma was advertised in the UK using footage and music lifted from which movie?

A. The French Connection

B. Bullitt

C. The Thomas Crown Affair

D. The Driver

## A5

Which car company used the guitar riff from the song "Layla" in its UK television advertisements?

A. Renault

B. Ford

C. Volkswagen

D. Vauxhall

## A6

Whose cars were promoted by the Scotland football team in 1978?

A. Ford

B. Vauxhall

C. British Leyland

D. Chrysler

## A7

Which car featured in a UK advertisement with the slogan "You can always say it's your wife's"?

A. VW Beetle Convertible

B. Citroën Dyane

C. Mazda MX-5

D. Fiat Panda

## A8

"The People's Ferrari" was a slogan used to advertise which British sports car in the USA?

A. Triumph TR7

B. Lotus Esprit

C. MG Midget

D. Triumph GT6

## A9

Which singing star appeared (and sang) in a UK TV commercial for the Chrysler Sunbeam?

A. Cilla Black

B. Dusty Springfield

C. Sandie Shaw

D. Petula Clark

## A10

Which Hollywood star appeared in the UK TV commercial for the Ford Cougar in the late 1990s?

A. Dennis Hopper

B. Jack Nicholson

C. Steve McQueen

D. James Garner

## General Knowledge V

### G41

What nickname was given to the Renault 14 in France?

A. L'ouef

B. La poire

C. Le fauteuil

D. La moutarde

### G42

What was the name of the rotary-engined Citroën that was based on the Ami 8?

A. M35

B. S16

C. X10

D. P19

### G43

What was the first production car to have a mid-mounted engine?

A. Lotus Europa

B. Bonnet Djet

C. Lamborghini Miura

D. De Tomaso Vallelunga

## G44

The Citroën DS is credited with saving the life of which political leader?

A. Idi Amin

B. Giscard D'Estaing

C. Francisco Franco

D. Charles De Gaulle

## G45

Which car was mentioned in a 1977 memo to President Jimmy Carter by his Assistant for National Security Affairs?

A. Bitter CD

B. Matra Rancho

C. Rover 3500

D. Renault 30 TX

## G46

What British car was fitted with a so-called *Quartic* steering wheel?

A. Princess

B. Morris Marina

C. Austin Maestro

D. Austin Allegro

## G47

Which French car company had a factory at Slough?

A. Citroën

B. Renault

C. Simca

D. Peugeot

## G48

The Alfa Romeo Arna was produced as a joint venture with which other car manufacturer?

A. Renault

B. Suzuki

C. SEAT

D. Nissan

## G49

Under what name was the Fiat Strada marketed in its native Italy?

A. Argenta

B. Stilo

C. Ritmo

D. Calcio

**G50**

Which of the following cars was not fitted with the PRV V6 engine?

A. Renault Safrane

B. Volvo 850

C. Citroen XM

D. Peugeot 605

## The People

### P1

Which political leader is said to have crashed his Rolls-Royce Silver Shadow into a truck?

A.  Leonid Brezhnev

B.  Idi Amin

C.  Gough Whitlam

D.  Edward Heath

### P2

Which motoring journalist ran a turbocharged Citroën 2CV in the 1980s?

A.  Peter Dron

B.  Mel Nichols

C.  Steve Cropley

D.  L.J.K. Setright

### P3

Who styled the Lotus Elite and Eclat models introduced in the mid-1970s?

A.  Trevor Fiore

B.  Oliver Winterbottom

C.  William Towns

D.  Ron Hickman

## P4

Music producer Giorgio Moroder was involved with the company that manufactured which supercar?

A. Bugatti EB110

B. Vector W8

C. Cizeta V16T

D. Isdera Imperator 108i

## P5

Which Lotus employee did much of the stunt driving of the Lotus Esprit in the 1977 film, *'The Spy Who Loved Me'*?

A. Mike Kimberly

B. Roger Becker

C. Warren King

D. John Miles

## P6

Which pop star crashed an Austin Maxi into a ditch on a trip to the Scottish highlands in 1969?

A. Paul McCartney

B. Mick Jagger

C. John Lennon

D. George Harrison

**P7**

What car was closely associated with Princess Anne during the 1970s and 1980s?

A. Triumph Stag

B. Jensen Interceptor

C. Reliant Scimitar GTE

D. Aston Martin V8 Volante

**P8**

Derek Robinson became infamous in the 1970s as a trade union official at which car manufacturer?

A. Chrysler

B. Vauxhall

C. Ford

D. British Leyland

**P9**

In 1983, which prominent UK politician survived a motorway crash that wrecked his brand new Ford Sierra?

A. Neil Kinnock

B. David Steel

C. Tony Benn

D. Michael Jopling

## P10

What car did Yuri Gagarin, the first human in space, receive as a gift from France in 1965?

A. Citroën DS Pallas

B. Alpine A110

C. Renault 8 Gordini

D. Matra-Bonnet Djet VS

# General Knowledge VI

## G51

The Ferrari 208 GTB and GTS were primarily intended for sale in which territory?

A. California

B. United Arab Emirates

C. Italy

D. Switzerland

## G52

The Panther 6 was so-called because...?

A. It had six wheels

B. It had six seats

C. It had a six-cylinder engine

D. It was the sixth model to have been produced by the company

## G53

What was the name of the four-wheeled Reliant that shared the same engine as the Robin?

A. Vixen

B. Kitten

C. Terrier

D. Wren

**G54**

What was the first mass-produced car to have a hot-dip galvanised chassis?

A. Talbot-Matra Murena

B. Porsche 944

C. Lotus Elan M100

D. Lancia Dedra

**G55**

Launched in 1980, the Fiat Panda was named after...?

A. A bear native to China

B. A Goddess

C. A species of butterfly

D. A coral island in the Caribbean Sea

**G56**

Which British engineering company produced the 'Tracer', an estate version of the Triumph TR7?

A. Torcars

B. Tickford

C. Overfinch

D. Crayford

## G57

Which Lancia was sold in the USA as the Scorpion?

A. Beta coupé

B. Beta HPE

C. Fulvia HF

D. Beta Montecarlo

## G58

Which company best known for sporting cars also built three-wheel invalid tricycles for the UK government?

A. Lotus

B. Jensen

C. AC

D. TVR

## G59

Which car gave rise to a limited edition 'Jeans' model (complete with denim seat covers) in the 1970s?

A. Fiat 127

B. Austin Mini

C. Citroën 2CV

D. VW Beetle

**G60**

The Hillman Avenger was sold in the USA as the …?

A. Dodge Polara

B. Plymouth Cricket

C. Plymouth Scamp

D. Chrysler Conquest

## Film & TV II

### F11

In what year was *'Top Gear'* first broadcast in the UK?

A.   1981

B.   1979

C.   1983

D.   1977

### F12

Which Hollywood film star raced a Mini in a round of the British Saloon Car Championship?

A.   Paul Newman

B.   James Garner

C.   Steve McQueen

D.   Gene Hackman

### F13

Who directed the classic 1984 TV advert for Shell that featured a Porsche 944, a quiet filling station and an empty road?

A.   David Putnam

B.   Tony Scott

C.   Hugh Hudson

D.   John Boorman

### F14

What car does the main character, Kowalski, drive in the 1971 film *'Vanishing Point'*?

A. AMC Javelin

B. Mercury Comet

C. Dodge Challenger R/T

D. Ford Maverick Sprint

### F15

In the film *'The Blues Brothers'*, what car is used by Jake and Elwood Blues?

A. Dodge Monaco

B. Ford LTD Crown Victoria

C. Chevrolet Nova

D. AMC Matador

### F16

What car was featured in the 1967 film, *'The Graduate'*?

A. Fiat 124 Spider

B. Alfa Romeo 1600 Spider

C. Lancia Aurelia Spider

D. Fiat Dino Spider

### F17

What car does the character played by Dennis Weaver drive in the film *'Duel'*?

A. Chevrolet Impala

B. Ford Fairmont

C. AMC Ambassador

D. Plymouth Valiant

### F18

In the TV series *'Return of the Saint'*, what car does the titular character drive?

A. Jaguar XJ-S

B. Volvo P1800

C. Triumph Dolomite Sprint

D. Jaguar XJ-C

### F19

In the 1975 James Bond film, *'The Man With The Golden Gun'*, what car performs a 270 degree roll whilst jumping over a river?

A. AMC Hornet X

B. Ford Mustang Mach One

C. Chevrolet Camaro

D. Plymouth Barracuda

## F20

What car, then owned by George Harrison, appears in the video for The Beatles' 1996 single '*Real Love*'?

A.  Aston Martin DB5

B.  Mercedes 500 SEL AMG

C.  Porsche 928 S2

D.  McLaren F1

## General Knowledge VII

### G61

On what car was the Fiat Barchetta based?

A. Fiat Punto

B. Lancia Delta

C. Alfa Romeo 145

D. Fiat Tipo

### G62

What colour was the Ford Mustang Steve McQueen drove in the film *Bullitt*?

A. Seafoam Green

B. Lime Gold

C. Highland Green

D. Forest Green

### G63

What was the name of the notchback saloon version of the Lancia Beta?

A. Thesis

B. Trevi

C. Thema

D. Dedra

**G64**

What engine was used to power Bill Collins's original DeLorean DMC-12 prototype?

A.  Renault 2.5 litre V6

B.  GM 2.5 litre 'Iron Duke'

C.  Citroën 2.2 litre

D.  Ford 2.0 litre 'Pinto'

**G65**

Which actress provided the voice used by the 'talking dashboard' of the early MG and Vanden Plas models of the Austin Maestro?

A.  Jan Harvey

B.  Nicolette McKenzie

C.  Judi Dench

D.  Maggie Smith

**G66**

The cheapest version of the TVR Tasmin was powered by which four-cylinder engine?

A.  Ford 2.0 litre 'Pinto'

B.  Triumph 2,0 litre 16V slant-four

C.  Vauxhall 2.3 litre slant-four

D.  BL 2.0 litre O-series

## G67

The Alfa Romeo SZ was given which nickname in Italy?

A. Il Brutto

B. Il Mattone

C. Il Mostro

D. Il Pugile

## G68

What vehicle formed the basis of the 'Popemobile' used during the Papal visit to Spain in 1982?

A. Citroën CX

B. Fiat Campagnola

C. Ford Granada

D. SEAT Panda

## G69

Lotus Elan designer Ron Hickman also designed which famous product?

A. Sodastream

B. Black & Decker WorkMate

C. Goblin Teasmade

D. Raleigh Chopper

**G70**

Which British car was sold in Italy as the Innocenti Regent?

A. Austin Allegro

B. Triumph Dolomite

C. Austin Princess

D. Morris Marina

# It's a Numbers Game II

## N11

In what year was the MGB first sold in the UK with rubber rather than chrome bumpers?

A. 1975

B. 1974

C. 1973

D. 1972

## N12

How many examples of the Citroën GS Birotor were built?

A. 847

B. 538

C. 903

D. 726

## N13

In what year did the Ford Cortina mark IV go on sale in in the UK?

A. 1976

B. 1979

C. 1975

D. 1980

## N14

In which year did it become compulsory in the UK for a front seat occupant of a car to wear a seat belt?

A.  1978

B.  1983

C.  1980

D.  1975

## N15

How many Vauxhall Belmonts were licensed in the UK as at the second quarter of 2020?

A.  31

B.  52

C.  17

D.  26

## N16

In what year did the Fiat X1/9 become the Bertone X1/9?

A.  1982

B.  1985

C.  1981

D.  1987

## N17

In January 1977 a Lotus Esprit cost £8051 on the road. How much did the corresponding model cost in June 1981?

A. £11,904

B. £13,513

C. £14,891

D. £10,186

## N18

In what year was the Triumph name last used on a new car?

A. 1982

B. 1984

C. 1986

D. 1988

## N19

In what year did the V12-powered Series 3 version of the Jaguar E-Type first go on sale in the UK?

A. 1968

B. 1973

C. 1970

D. 1971

**N20**

The Vignale-styled Fiat Samantha coupé was based on which model?

A.   128

B.   124

C.   127

D.   125

## General Knowledge VIII

### G71

Why was production of the Lancia Beta Montecarlo stopped for two years?

A.An energy crisis had affected sales

B.Its engine suffered from overheating issues

C.Its brakes were prone to locking-up

D.The factory it was built in was heavily damaged by fire

### G72

A special edition of which car was produced to celebrate Italy's hosting of the 1990 football world cup?

A.Lancia Delta

B.Fiat Uno

C.Alfa Romeo 33

D.Fiat Panda

### G73

What was the first hot hatchback?

A.Renault 5 TS

B.Simca 1100 TI

C.Fiat 128 3P

D.Peugeot 104 ZS

## G74

In which British Leyland factory was the Triumph TR7 **not** built?

A. Speke

B. Longbridge

C. Solihull

D. Canley

## G75

What car was the subject of the first chapter of Ralph Nader's book, *'Unsafe at any Speed'*?

A. NSU Prinz

B. Volkswagen Beetle

C. Chevrolet Corvair

D. AMC Gremlin

## G76

Which fashion designer created a 'designer edition' of the Matra-Simca Bagheera sports car?

A. Ted Lapidus

B. Sergio Tacchini

C. André Courrèges

D. Yves Saint Laurent

## G77

The Ecosse Signature was based on which British sports car?

A. MGB GT V8

B. AC 3000 ME

C. TVR Taimar

D. Lotus Elan

## G78

For which of these American car manufacturers did John Z. De Lorean **not** work?

A. Chrysler

B. Ford

C. General Motors

D. Packard

## G79

Which company owned Citroën prior to Peugeot's acquisition of it in 1976?

A. Renault

B. Elf

C. Aérospatiale

D. Michelin

## G80

*'Autocar & Motor'* advised their readers to sell "your grandmother and the rest of your family, your dog, your cat and anything else to hand" in order to have which car?

A. Mazda MX-5

B. BMW M3 (E30)

C. Lotus Elan M100

D. Lancia integrale

# Part Two: The Answers

## *General Knowledge I*

| | | |
|---|---|---|
| G1 | B. | Ford |
| G2 | A. | Renault 11 |
| G3 | B. | 10 |
| G4 | C. | Alfa Romeo 1900 |
| G5 | A. | VW Beetle |
| G6 | D. | P76 |
| G7 | A. | Porsche 914 |
| G8 | C. | 1949 |
| G9 | C. | Lancia Delta |
| G10 | B. | 1300/1500 |

# *Film & TV I*

| | | |
|---|---|---|
| F1  | C. | Target |
| F2  | A. | Dodge M4S |
| F3  | C. | BMW 323i Baur Cabriolet |
| F4  | D. | Citroën SM |
| F5  | A. | Bond Bug |
| F6  | B. | Ford Zodiac |
| F7  | A. | Austin A60 Cambridge |
| F8  | C. | 88 miles per hour |
| F9  | C. | Ford Probe |
| F10 | D. | DBS |

# General Knowledge II

| | | |
|---|---|---|
| G11 | B. | Ford Escort |
| G12 | B. | Continuously Variable Transmission |
| G13 | C. | 1982 |
| G14 | B. | Citroën |
| G15 | B. | Rover |
| G16 | D. | Audi 50 |
| G17 | A. | Suzuki Cappuccino |
| G18 | A. | Scamp |
| G19 | B. | Renault 16 |
| G20 | D. | They share their name with a wind |

# It's a Numbers Game I

| | | |
|---|---|---|
| N1 | D. | 23 |
| N2 | B. | 3878 |
| N3 | B. | 1973 |
| N4 | A. | 9 |
| N5 | C. | 115,041 |
| N6 | C. | 3500cc |
| N7 | A. | 1978 |
| N8 | C. | 1979 |
| N9 | B. | 1980 |
| N10 | C. | 557 |

# *General Knowledge III*

| | | |
|---|---|---|
| G21 | C. | Lamborghini |
| G22 | C. | Paykan |
| G23 | A. | Daihatsu Compagno |
| G24 | C. | Rubery Owen |
| G25 | D. | Lonsdale |
| G26 | C. | Midship Runabout |
| G27 | A. | Daytona |
| G28 | B. | 345 |
| G29 | B. | BMW Z1 |
| G30. | A. | A guided missile |

# *Motorsport*

| M1 | A. | Hillman Hunter |
|---|---|---|
| M2 | C. | Keke Rosberg |
| M3 | A. | USA |
| M4 | C. | Citroën DS 21 |
| M5 | B. | Audi 80 GLE |
| M6 | A. | Hillman/Chrysler Avenger |
| M7 | B. | Citroën BX |
| M8 | C. | Lancia 037 |
| M9 | B. | Opel Ascona 400 |
| M10 | A. | Triumph TR6 |

# General Knowledge IV

| | | |
|---|---|---|
| G31 | D. | K70 |
| G32 | B. | It had a gas turbine engine |
| G33 | B. | Spain |
| G34 | D. | Sonett |
| G35 | A. | Morris Ital |
| G36 | A. | Ford Cortina 1600E |
| G37 | B. | Arizona |
| G38 | C. | BMW 2002 Turbo |
| G39 | A. | Peel P50 |
| G40 | D. | Ford Corsair |

## It Pays To Advertise

| | | |
|---|---|---|
| A1 | A. | Princess 2 |
| A2 | B. | Citroën AX GT |
| A3 | C. | Ford Capri |
| A4 | B. | Bullitt |
| A5 | D. | Vauxhall |
| A6 | D. | Chrysler |
| A7 | B. | Citroën Dyane |
| A8 | C. | MG Midget |
| A9 | D. | Petula Clark |
| A10 | A. | Dennis Hopper |

# General Knowledge V

| | | |
|---|---|---|
| G41 | B. | La poire |
| G42 | A. | M35 |
| G43 | B. | Bonnet Djet |
| G44 | D. | Charles De Gaulle |
| G45 | B. | Matra Rancho |
| G46 | D. | Austin Allegro |
| G47 | A. | Citroën |
| G48 | D. | Nissan |
| G49 | C. | Ritmo |
| G50 | B. | Volvo 850 |

# *The People*

| | | |
|---|---|---|
| P1 | A. | Leonid Brezhnev |
| P2 | C. | Steve Cropley |
| P3 | B. | Oliver Winterbottom |
| P4 | C. | Cizeta V16T |
| P5 | B. | Roger Becker |
| P6 | C. | John Lennon |
| P7 | C. | Reliant Scimitar GTE |
| P8 | D. | British Leyland |
| P9 | A. | Neil Kinnock |
| P10 | D. | Matra-Bonnet Djet VS |

# General Knowledge VI

G51   C.   Italy

G52   A.   It had six wheels

G53   B.   Kitten

G54   A.   Talbot-Matra Murena

G55   B.   A Goddess

G56   D.   Crayford

G57   D.   Beta Montecarlo

G58   C.   AC

G59   D.   VW Beetle

G60   B.   Plymouth Cricket

# *Film & TV II*

| | | |
|---|---|---|
| F11 | D. | 1977 |
| F12 | C. | Steve McQueen |
| F13 | B. | Tony Scott |
| F14 | C. | Dodge Challenger R/T |
| F15 | A. | Dodge Monaco |
| F16 | B. | Alfa-Romeo 1600 Spider |
| F17 | D. | Plymouth Valiant |
| F18 | A. | Jaguar XJ-S |
| F19 | A. | AMC Hornet X |
| F20 | B. | Mercedes 500 SEL AMG |

## *General Knowledge VII*

| | | |
|---|---|---|
| G61 | A. | Fiat Panda |
| G62 | C. | Highland Green |
| G63 | B. | Trevi |
| G64 | C. | Citroën 2.2 litre |
| G65 | B. | Nicolette McKenzie |
| G66 | A. | Ford 2.0 litre 'Pinto' |
| G67 | C. | Il Mostro |
| G68 | D. | SEAT Panda |
| G69 | B. | Black & Decker WorkMate |
| G70 | A. | Austin Allegro |

# It's a Numbers Game II

| | | |
|---|---|---|
| N11 | B. | 1974 |
| N12 | A. | 847 |
| N13 | A | 1976 |
| N14 | B. | 1983 |
| N15 | C. | 17 |
| N16 | A. | 1982 |
| N17 | B. | £13,513 |
| N18 | B. | 1984 |
| N19 | D. | 1971 |
| N20 | D. | 125 |

## General Knowledge VIII

G71   C.   Its brakes were prone to locking-up

G72   D.   Fiat Panda

G73   B.   Simca 1100 TI

G74   B.   Longbridge

G75   C.   Chevrolet Corvair

G76   C.   André Courrèges

G77   B.   AC 3000 ME

G78   B.   Ford

G79   D.   Michelin

G80   C.   Lotus Elan M100

# Part Three: The Stories Behind The Answers

Quizzes are fun, but they're even better when they inform as well as entertain.

With that in mind, this section contains stories (for want of a better word) that in some way relate to each corresponding question.

Some of the stories are brief, others rather less so. Between them, they contain a mixture of facts, statistics, trivia, the occasional flippant remark and one or two bits of reasonable speculation.

And, yes, the story about the Hollywood film star and the BSCC is true…

# General Knowledge I

## G1

*Edsel was a short-lived brand owned by which company?*

**B.     Ford**

Named after Edsel Ford, the son of company founder Henry Ford, Edsel was launched in 1957 as the third branch of the Lincoln-Mercury division of Ford Motor Company.

Edsel was launched with a range of four saloons and three station wagons, all sharing their platforms and running gear with other models in the Ford stable. Edsels did, however, come with a few novelties, including a speed warning system, a rotating, dome-type speedometer; and optional push-button *Teletouch* automatic transmission, the buttons for which were mounted on the steering hub.

Ford entertained high hopes for the Edsel brand, even commissioning a special TV programme, *The Edsel Show*, to promote it. Those hopes were, however, quickly dashed, as customers stayed away in droves.

The first and most visible reason for buyer apathy was the ugliness of the Edsel corporate grille, which looked like an elongated toilet seat. Ford eventually changed the grille for a more aesthetically pleasing design, but by then the writing was on the wall for the brand.

Other factors which adversely affected the brand's chances of success included issues with build quality and Ford's miscalculation as to Edsel's place in the Ford range. Intended to sit between Ford and Mercury in terms of pricing and brand prestige, Edsel found itself occupying No Man's Land rather than an identifiable market niche. Moreover, the brand's lack of identity was compounded by the fact that Edsel didn't have a separate production facility from Ford and Mercury.

And just to add to Edsel's difficulties, the US economy went into recession shortly after the brand's launch. This drove customers towards smaller, cheaper cars and away from Edsels.

Sales peaked in 1958 but never came close to meeting the break-even point let alone matching Ford's projections. The plug was pulled on the brand in November 1959, with production ceasing at the end of that month after 116,000 examples had been built.

Ford lost an estimated $250,000,000 on the Edsel project, which equates to about $2.2 billion in today's money. Ouch!

## G2

*In the 1985 film 'A View to a Kill', what car does James Bond commandeer in Paris?*

**A.     Renault 11**

One of the most enjoyable things about watching older films is that it affords the opportunity to look at cars which were once a common sight but are now rarely, if ever, seen.

The 1985 James Bond movie, *A View to a Kill*, is no exception to this. It's far from being the best Bond film but the sequences filmed in Paris make it a good one for car-spotting, particularly if you like French cars of the 70s and early 80s.

The film actually has two car chase sequences, but we'll concentrate on the one in which Bond 'borrows' a phase 1 Renault 11 TXE from a taxi driver and embarks on a pursuit through the streets, pavements, stairways and embankments of Paris. Mind you, having enjoyed a few taxi rides in Paris, I reckon he might have done better to hire the taxi and let the driver get on with it. Either that or nicked the grippier and more powerful 11 Turbo model...

Ah well, c'est la vie.

## G3

*When introduced in 1960, the UK MOT test applied to cars of what minimum age (in years)?*

**B.    10**

The MOT test was rolled out in 1960 as a test of basic roadworthiness for cars of ten years old or over.

For the first few months after its introduction, owners of cars of the appropriate age could choose whether or not to submit their vehicles for testing. That changed in early 1961, when the MOT test became compulsory for all cars aged ten or more.

Due to the high number of vehicles that failed the test, the age-limit was changed to seven years on 31st December 1961 and was subsequently reduced to three years in 1967.

The scope of the MOT test has changed over time, with checks on tyres, emissions, horns, indicators, wipers and various other components having all being added.

A significant change came in 2005, when the MOT database was computerised. Instead of the watermarked, A5 size MOT certificates previously issued, people presenting their cars for testing received an unwatermarked sheet of A4 paper, with the salient information (i.e.pass, fail, advisories) from each test being uploaded to a publicly accessible website.

### G4

*The BAT 5, BAT 7 and BAT 9 concept cars of the 1950s were all based on which chassis?*

**C.    Alfa Romeo 1900**

They may sound like something from an American comic strip, but the three BAT concept cars are thoroughly Italian.

The fruit of an Alfa Romeo-commissioned project to create a car with the lowest possible drag factor, the three BAT (*Berlinetta Aerodinamica Tecnica*) cars were designed and built by Bertone on Alfa Romeo 1900 chassis.

The three cars that emerged – BAT 5 in 1953, BAT 7 in 1954 and BAT 9 in 1955 - made extensive use of rounded edges and curved fins, giving them the appearance of something out of a Hollywood science fiction film. Moreover, they were aerodynamically efficient, with BAT 7, the slipperiest of the three, having a drag factor of just 0.19.

All three of the 1950s BATs still exist, and in 2008 Alfa Romeo and Bertone joined forces once more to create the Alfa 8C Competitzione-based BAT 11.

## G5

*Which European car was advertised in the USA with the slogan "Think Small"?*

**A.  VW Beetle**

Although it was never built in the USA, the Volkswagen Beetle sold there in the millions.

The Beetle started slowly in the USA, but from 1955 onwards its sales increased year after year, reaching their zenith in 1968, when almost 400,000 Beetles were sold in a single year.

It was neither fast nor luxurious, and it most certainly wasn't the last word in style and sophistication. Instead, it sold because it was affordable, reliable and easy to work on. It was also brilliantly marketed by means of a string of clear, simple and perfectly pitched advertisements that highlighted the Beetle's qualities without veering into hyperbole.

Perhaps the most significant of all the ads VW commissioned for the Beetle was the 1959 "Think Small" advertisement created by copywriter Julian Koenig and art director Helmut Krone of the Doyle Dane Bernach agency. Printed in black and white, it was a masterpiece of simplicity that exuded honesty.

The ad was a huge success with the American public. More importantly, an ever-increasing number of Americans went out and purchased a Beetle. It set the template for future Volkswagen advertisements in the

USA and played a significant part in persuading Americans to take the slow, funny-looking little German car to their hearts.

## G6

*What was the name of the Michelotti-designed saloon built by Leyland Australia but never sold in the UK?*

**D.     P76**

Launched in 1973, the P76 was Leyland (yes, *that* Leyland) Australia's attempt at building a large car specifically aimed at the Australian market.

Styled by Michelotti, the P76 looked less like an Italian thoroughbred in working clothes than a supersized 1970s Datsun; it was not a handsome car. On the other hand, it had a decent specification, enjoyed a weight advantage over its similarly-sized competitors and offered a choice of two engines: a 2.6 litre straight six and a 4.4 litre V8, the latter being derived from the 3.5 litre unit used by Rover in the UK.

The P76 got off to a good start, with the V8 version taking *Wheels* magazine's Car of the Year award, but its progress was arrested by the poor build quality of early examples, strikes at component suppliers and the effect of the global energy crisis of 1973/4.

Against this backdrop, sales failed to meet expectations, and plans to add a station wagon and a coupé, named Force 7, to the range never came to fruition. Leyland had also intended to import the P76 into the UK, but this too fell by the wayside.

Production ceased in Australia in late 1974, although assembly of P76s from CKD (Complete Knock Down) kits continued in New Zealand until 1976.

Just over 18,000 P76s were built along with several pre-production Force 7 coupés and three prototype station wagons (two of which were destroyed for testing and certification purposes). Its short production life notwithstanding, the P76 has a loyal following in both Australia and New Zealand.

# G7

*What was the first car to be used as the Safety Car in an F1 Grand Prix?*

## A.     Porsche 914

There was a time when Formula 1 Grands Prix continued even whilst rescue and recovery attempts were ongoing after crashes.

The 1973 season was a particularly bad year* for crashes, the most tragic example of this being the 1973 Dutch Grand Prix, in which the race continued whilst driver David Purley and some poorly-equipped marshals vainly tried to extricate Roger Williamson from the blazing wreckage of his March.

It took until 1993 for F1 to fully embrace the idea of a Safety Car, but the first use of one came 20 years earlier in the 1973 Canadian Grand Prix.

The track was wet when the race started, so wet in fact that the drivers were permitted three exploratory laps before forming up on the grid. There were a few spins and crashes in the early stages of the race, but as the track dried another problem emerged: the wet tyres fitted to most of the cars were overheating and losing their tread. Chaos then ensued as car after car came in to pit for new tyres, but the biggest incident occurred on lap 32 when Jody Scheckter's McLaren collided with the Tyrrell of Francois Cevert, putting both out of the race and littering the track with debris.

At this juncture, the organisers sent out a Safety Car, a yellow Porsche 914 driven by racing driver Eppie Wietzes, with Peter Mackintosh of the Formula One Constructors' Association aboard as co-driver. With Mackintosh taking instructions by radio from race control, Wietzes picked up the car of Howden Ganley, having mistakenly been told that he was the leader. Wietzes thereafter led Ganley and the rest of the field around the circuit at a modest pace until racing resumed five laps later.

Unfortunately, the failure of race control to pick out the correct leader compounded the chaos caused by the multitude of pit stops and resulted in a situation in which no one really knew who the leader was. Indeed, it wasn't until an hour after the race ended that Peter Revson was declared the winner, an outcome that is still argued over to this day.

But although the Safety Car had inadvertently added to the confusion, it unquestionably helped to keep track workers and drivers safe in challenging conditions.

* Two British drivers (Mike Hailwood and David Purley) were awarded the George Medal that year for their respective actions in going to the aid of drivers trapped in blazing F1 cars.

## G8

*In what year did the Citroën 2CV go into production?*

**C.    1949**

But for World War 2, the Citroën 2CV would have reached the market almost a decade earlier than it did.

Its story began in 1934, when Citroën started to explore the creation of a cheap, reliable and durable car largely aimed at France's large rural population. The car had to be able to carry four people and their wares across unpaved roads and rutted fields whilst offering excellent fuel economy.

The result of this was the TPV (Toute Petit Voiture, or very small car), a utilitarian car with supple suspension, a spartan interior and single headlamp. From these prototypes came a run of 250 pre-production cars with 700cc water-cooled flat-twin engines, front-wheel drive, four doors and a fabric roof.

The TPV prototypes were crudely finished – the front end, from the scuttle to the bumper, was fashioned out of corrugated metal – but the basic shape was one that millions of people would come to know well. Their interior was basic too, with a dash-mounted lever for the three-speed manual transmission, and seat backs held in place by wires attached to the roof pillars.

Plans were made to show the TPV at the Paris Motor Show in October 1939. However, the advent of the Second World War resulted in the cancellation of the show. A few months later, with the invading German forces sweeping all before them, almost all of the TPV prototypes were destroyed.

Citroën quietly continued to develop the TPV during the war. Various changes were made to its specification, not the least of which was the replacement of the water-cooled engine used in the prototypes with an air-cooled unit.

When production began in 1949, the demand for the 2CV proved that Citroën had got it right. Over the years, it came to play a hugely important role in the lives of France's rural population, offering flexible and affordable transport for them, their families and their produce. Indeed, it wouldn't be an exaggeration to say that the 2CV transformed the lives of many of its buyers.

As a concept it was so perfectly judged that its basic design changed little over its 41 years in production.

It is arguably the most important car not only of its time but of any era.

## G9

*The Saab 600 of the early 1980s was a rebadged...?*

### C.    Lancia Delta

Between 1980 and 1982 the Lancia Delta was sold in Sweden, Norway, Denmark, and Finland as the Saab-Lancia 600.

At first blush, it seems strange that Saab, a company with a reputation for building hardy, albeit somewhat stolid, cars should link up with Lancia, whose products tended to be stylish, exciting...and fragile.

Delve a little deeper, though, and the background reveals itself. Saab's elderly 93 and 96 models were due to be pensioned off and the company had no mid-sized car with which to replace them. Moreover, Saab was keen on adding an executive saloon to its range, but the cost of developing a new model was prohibitive.

The solution to both problems came in 1978, when they entered into an agreement with Fiat, who were equally keen to develop new executive saloons for both Fiat and Lancia. That took care not only of the executive saloon project but, in 1980, also enabled Saab to offer a new mid-sized car in the form of a rebadged Lancia Delta.

Known as the Saab-Lancia 600, the rebranded Delta was only ever offered with a 1.5 litre engine and in three (later two) trim levels. Sales began in 1980 and ended two years later, the anticipated level of sales not having materialised. Aside from the reluctance of Scandinavian and Finnish customers to buy a car made by a manufacturer with a reputation for dubious build quality, the price of the 600 was too high - it wasn't very much cheaper than the Saab 99.

Saab's joint executive car project with Fiat was, however, rather more successful. It gave rise to the Type 4 platform on which the Saab 9000, Fiat Croma, Lancia Thema and Alfa Romeo 164 (Fiat acquired Alfa in 1986) were based.

## G10

*Which of the following Triumph cars has front-wheel drive?*

**B.     1300/1500**

Launched in 1965, the Michelotti-designed Triumph 1300 was the first front-wheel drive car produced by the Leyland-owned marque.

In the early 1960s, Leyland's rival, BMC, was enjoying considerable success with the Mini and the Austin 1100, both of which featured front-wheel drive. It seemed logical, therefore, for Triumph to employ this drivetrain configuration on the 1300.

There was, however, one difference between the BMC cars and the Triumph 1300: in the BMC cars, the engine was mounted transversely whereas in the Triumph it was mounted longitudinally, a configuration that was somewhat less space-efficient.

The 1300 had a good specification for its time, with all-round independent suspension, front disc brakes and an adjustable steering column. However, it was unable to compete with the cheaper BMC 1100 in so far as sales were concerned – indeed, more 1100s were sold in the UK in one year* than the entire number of Triumph 1300s built.

In 1968, BMC and Leyland merged. Although production of both the BMC 1100/1300 (the larger-engined model appeared in 1967) and Triumph 1300 continued, the latter's development thereafter took an unexpected turn.

The 1300 was joined by a new 1500 model in 1970. The 1300 remained unchanged but the 1500 had a restyled nose and tail, bigger boot and different dashboard. But while those changes were for the better, the decision to give the 1500 a dead beam rear axle rather than carry over the 1300's independent rear suspension set-up was a step backwards.

Of rather more significance, however, was the release the same year of a new rear-wheel drive model, the Triumph Toledo. In essence, the Toledo was a re-engineered, lightly restyled, rear-wheel drive version of the 1300/1500. More pertinently, it was cheaper. The introduction of the Toledo was followed by a larger-engined, more upmarket version, the Dolomite, in 1973.

This spelled the end of the road for the 1500, the 1300 having been dropped in 1971. Moreover, it marked the end of Triumph's foray into front-wheel drive; thereafter, all home-grown Triumphs - the early 1980s Acclaim was a rebadged Honda Ballade - would drive only their rear wheels.

* Around 148,500 examples of the Triumph 1300 and 1300 TC were built from 1965 to 1971. By way of comparison, the BMC 1100 sold over 150,000 examples in the UK in both 1965 and 1966.

# Film & TV

## F1

*In which 1985 film did a Peugeot 205 GTI feature in a car chase?*

### C.     Target

The 205 GTI was still something of a novelty when the Gene Hackman/Matt Dillon thriller *Target* was filmed.

In the film, Hackman and Dillon rent a silver* 205 GTI 1.6. A Renault 20 follows them and a car chase develops, in which the pursuing Renault appears to pass the same Citroën GS several times...

The chase itself is fairly tame by most standards, although the stunt driver at the wheel of the 205 didoes a good job of putting it through its paces.

It's a decent enough film, truth be told, and definitely one to catch if you're a fan of the 205 GTI. But even if you're not, enough interesting French and German (filming took place in both countries) cars appear on screen to make for a good game of classic car I-spy.

* A silver 205 GTI also features in a car chase in the 1985 French film, *Subway*. What's that they say about great minds thinking alike...

## F2

*The 'Turbo Interceptor' in the 1986 film 'The Wraith' was based on which concept car?*

### A.     Dodge M4S

The best thing about this 1986 Charlie Sheen movie is the titular character's 'Turbo Interceptor', a low-slung, streamlined coupé that's powered by, well, your guess is as good as mine.

And although it may seem unlikely at first glance, the Turbo Interceptor is based on an actual car, the Dodge M4S.

The M4S owes its existence to PPG, the title sponsors of the CART Indy Car World Series in the 1980s. To help promote the series, PPG worked with car manufacturers to produce prototype or modified cars to act as pace cars at races. The M4S was one such car. .

Designed by Dodge's Bob Ackerman, work on the M4S (*Mid-engine, Four-cylinder, Sport*) began in 1983. Built around a spaceframe chassis, the streamlined (its drag factor was 0.236) M4S was powered by a twin-turbo 2.2 litre Chrysler engine with a power output of 440 bhp. It didn't quite attain the 200mph that Bob Ackerman hoped for, but its measured top speed of 194.8mph was nonetheless extremely impressive.

The M4S went on to appear as a pace car at several IndyCar races in 1986, but before that happened it had a date with the company filming *The Wraith*. The M4S was present on the film set for a time but doesn't actually appear in the finished film. Rather, the Turbo Interceptor is portrayed on screen by buggy-based replicas of the M4S.

### F3

*In the 1984 British film 'Comfort and Joy', what car does the main character, Alan 'Dickie' Bird, drive?*

### C.     BMW 323i Baur Cabriolet

If you're a fan of the lovely E30 Baur Cabriolet then perhaps you should give *Comfort and Joy* a miss. Sure, it's a great film, better in my opinion that Bill Forsyth's previous offering, *Local Hero*, but Alan 'Dickie' Bird's 323i Cabriolet doesn't half come in for some grief.

Played by the excellent Bill Paterson, Dickie Bird is justifiably proud of his 323i. But pride, as they say, comes before a fall. And in the case of Dickie's 323i, it all starts to go wrong when its owner witnesses thugs attack an ice cream van. Next thing Dickie knows, the velour seats of his beloved Beemer are covered with upside-down ice-cream cones, and it all goes downhill from there.

I won't tell you what happens thereafter but suffice it to say that the film uses the ever-worsening condition of Dickie's car as a running joke.

Besides, it's a film that deserves to be seen and enjoyed. So forget my previous warning and check it out, even if E30 Baur Cabriolets are dear to you.

## F4

*In the 1974 film 'The Longest Yard', what car does Burt Reynolds dump in the river?*

D.     **Citroën SM**

When it first appeared in 1970, the Citroën SM was like no other car on the road, both to look at and to drive. After all, how many other cars could claim to combine a quad-cam Maserati V6 engine with speed-sensitive, self-centring, power steering, hydropneumatic suspension and a zero-travel brake pedal that looked like a mushroom?

A perfect fit for a science-fiction film, then? Probably, but its most memorable outing was in the Burt Reynolds comedy, *The Longest Yard.*

The SM appears early in the film, when an inebriated Paul Crewe (Reynolds) steals it from his girlfriend, who shouts "Don't take my Maserati!" Crewe then leads the police on a wild chase before dumping the by now somewhat battered SM into a river*.

The SM was subsequently fished out of the water and sold by the producer for $7000. It's said that Reynolds liked the SM so much that he purchased one – not the one that had been in the river, mind - for his then partner, Dinah Shore.

*Eagle-eyed viewers will note that the SM driven by Reynolds has manual transmission which magically turns into an automatic version so that he can send it riverward by snicking the gear selector into 'Drive'.

## F5

*Luke Skywalker's landspeeder in the film 'Star Wars' was based on the chassis of which car?*

A.     **Bond Bug**

Yes, you read that right – Luke Skywalker's landspeeder was based on a three-wheeled car made in England, albeit one that is cool and funky in its own right.

The work required to turn the Bug into an X38 landspeeder was carried out under the supervision of the Bug's designer, Tom Karen of Ogle Design. The resulting 'landspeeder' had both steering and an engine and could move under its own power.

Brilliant though Tom Karen is, even he could not create a floating car. But that's where production designer and set decorator Roger Christian came in. To create the illusion of hovering, Christian fixed angled mirrors to the underside of the landspeeder. He then secured a brush to the landspeeder's chassis so that it would throw up dust as it moved. That's how they rolled in the days before CGI.

The Bond Bug may not be quite as cool as a landspeeder, but it's nonetheless a wonderfully idiosyncratic car in its own right: a three wheeled coupé with a lift-up canopy and side screens instead of doors. Oh, and you can have it in any colour you desire…as long as that colour is tangerine*.

The Bug was built by Reliant (who had taken over Bond in 1969) from 1970 to 1974. In all, 2268 Bugs were produced, the vast majority of them being powered by Reliant's 700cc four-cylinder engine.

It continues to have a dedicated following to this day. Indeed, as at the second quarter of 2020, more Bugs (159) were licensed with the DVLA than at any other time in the last 25 years.

*Six Bugs were produced in white for a tobacco company. It's believed that three of them still exist.

## F6

*The futuristic car driven by Ed Straker in the 1970 TV series 'UFO' was based on the chassis of which car?*

## B. Ford Zodiac

Gerry Anderson's first live-action TV series was imaginative if nothing else. It envisioned a 1980 in which Earth was under attack from UFOs capable of hyperlight speed and whose crews wore helmets filled with a green liquid.

Not that Earth was taking the threat lightly: a secret earth defence force (SHADO), whose HQ lay beneath a film studio, operated a moon base equipped with vertical take-off interceptors armed with large nuclear missiles.

SHADO's Earth defences weren't lacking either: there was a fleet of submarines with attached jet fighters capable of taking off underwater, a fleet of tracked mobiles ready to be deployed in any part of the world, and a sophisticated command and control set up. Oh, and the key figures in SHADO all drove futuristic cars powered by what sounds like gas turbine engines.

Unlike most of the props used in the series, the cars were real. Originally made for – and seen in – Anderson's film, *Journey to the Far Side of the Sun* (also known as *Doppelgänger*), they were designed by Derek Meddings and built by Alan Mann Racing on Ford Zodiac chassis. They were capable of moving under their own power, although the gull-wing doors had to be lifted manually, not that you'd know it from the TV series.

Three cars were built, two of which were used in *UFO*. When the series ended, the cars were used for promotional work and one of them – the car driven on-screen by Ed Straker, the commander of SHADO - was owned for a time by a Radio One DJ. Alas, it ended up in the back garden of a house, battered, tattered and beyond salvation. However, a fan of the show was able to make bodywork moulds from the car with the intention of producing a replica.

A legion of fans awaits its completion.

## F7

*In the 1969 film 'The Italian Job', what car falls off a car transporter onto a parked police car?*

**A.     Austin A60 Cambridge**

It occupies only a few seconds of screen time, but the scene in which the harassed police chief's car is wrecked by a falling car never fails to produce a laugh or two.

You might think that with the sequence in question having been filmed in Turin that the producers would have chosen an Italian car for the transporter scene. They did no such thing. Instead, as befits the film's cheerful Euro-scepticism, the police chief's Alfa Romeo Giulia is flattened by a very rusty Austin A60 Cambridge.

## F8

*In the 1985 film 'Back to the Future', what speed does Doc Brown's modified De Lorean have to reach in order to achieve time travel?*

**C.     88 miles per hour**

There's no particular significance in the figure of 88 miles per hour, so the most likely reason that the filmmakers chose it relates to the digital speed display in Doc Brown's DMC-12 - if you think about it, the numeral '8' uses the full matrix in an LED display and therefore looks more dramatic on screen.

As an aside, if the DeLorean used by the filmmakers was one of the early ones imported to the USA, they'd have had to replace its analogue speedometer if they'd wanted to use that to show the car's speed rather than go to the bother of adding a digital speed display.

Why?

The answer is that a Bill passed in 1979 required all new cars sold in the USA to be fitted with speedometers on which speed was calibrated only up to a maximum of 85 miles per hour, this being at a time when the national speed limit was 55 miles per hour.

President Reagan repealed the law relating to speedometers in 1981, but the Federally-mandated speed limit of 55 miles per hour lasted until 1995.

In any event, with just 130bhp on tap in Federal form, it would have taken a standard DMC-12 quite a while (28 seconds in automatic guise, a little less in manual form) to hit 88mph from rest.

## F9

*What car does Gareth Cheeseman drive in Steve Coogan's comedy, 'Dearth of a Salesman'?*

**C.     Ford Probe**

Back in the mid-1990s, Steve Coogan co-wrote and starred in *Coogan's Run,* a series of short, one-off TV comedies.

Of the six programmes that made up the series, the most memorable for car nuts was *Dearth of a Salesman*, in which Gareth Cheeseman, an egocentric, obnoxious computer hardware salesman, attends a sales conference in his blue Ford Probe.

Although the Probe only appears at the beginning and end of the show, it nonetheless became inextricably associated with the appalling Cheeseman, doing its credibility no good whatsoever. That said, it would be wrong to attribute the Probe's failure in the UK market to its role in a *Dearth of a Salesman.*

Its failure was more to do with its high price, iffy build quality and unfortunate name (what *were* the marketing people at Ford thinking...). It didn't help either that it was really a Mazda MX-6 in a party frock rather than a true-blue Ford. For the Probe, Gareth Cheeseman was just the runny icing on a cake that had failed to rise.

# F10

*What model of Aston Martin does Lord Brett Sinclair drive in* the TV series, *'The Persuaders'?*

**D.    DBS**

The world was a bigger place five decades ago, before cheap air travel became the rule rather than the exception. For many people, a taste of the exotic could only be sampled through films and TV programmes such as *The Persuaders*.

First shown in 1971, the series brought together Roger Moore and Tony Curtis as a pair of globe-trotting playboys who team up to fight crime. Much of the show was filmed on locations throughout Europe, thereby bringing a little glamour and glitz into British homes.

But it's the cars that we're interested in, and in this *The Persuaders* does not disappoint. Moore, as Lord Brett Sinclair, cuts around in a Bahama Yellow Aston Martin DBS (albeit with wheels and badging from the DBS V8 model), and Curtis can be found at the helm of a red, left-hand drive Dino 246GT.

Both cars were loaned to the TV production company: the DBS by Aston Martin and the Dino by its Italian owner. The Aston covered around 5000 miles during filming for the series. It was thereafter returned to Aston Martin and sold, still sporting the DBS V8 wheels and badges. It remains in the UK and retains the registration number it carried in the series. The Dino was also returned to its owner, who kept it for several years before moving it on. It is understood to remain in Italy but no longer carries the same registration mark as in the series.

# General Knowledge II

## G11

*What was the UK's best-selling car of the 1980s?*

**B.     Ford Escort**

Given that the Ford Cortina was, by some margin, the UK's best-selling car in the 1970s, it would be reasonable to assume that its successor, the Ford Sierra, emulated that feat in the 1980s.

It didn't.

Whereas the Cortina had topped the annual sales charts every year from 1972 to 1981, the Sierra never once did so. The Cortina's place as the nation's biggest-selling car was instead taken by the Ford Escort, its success mirroring that of the BMC 1100/1300 in the 1960s and early 1970s, when it was a mid-sized car that generated the most sales.

The Sierra's cause wasn't by aided by looks which alienated some potential buyers, its reliance on rear-wheel drive when its main rivals had switched to front-wheel drive, and, in the Escort, a marque rival that offered enough space for most families, looked better and had front-wheel drive.

After a couple of lean years, when it was outsold not only by the Escort but also by the Vauxhall Cavalier, the Sierra performed much better, its marketability having been enhanced by the addition of a booted saloon version, the Sierra Sapphire. Even so, it never once managed to outsell the Escort over a calendar year.

The Sierra was replaced by the Mondeo in 1993. It too failed to reach the number one position in the UK sales chart. Indeed, its sales fell away sharply over time, as the increasing size of smaller cars made them a viable - and more economical - proposition for many buyers.

As for the Escort, both it and its successor, the Ford Focus, continued to regularly, albeit not invariably, top the sales charts for some years to come. But in the same way that the Escort replaced the Cortina as the best-selling car, so too has the Focus been supplanted by a smaller (but considerably larger than it used to be) model, the Fiesta.

### G12

*What feature did the Volvo 343 have as standard when launched in 1976?*

**B.    Continuously Variable Transmission**

Had destiny taken another path, the Volvo 343 would have been known as the DAF 77.

Its story began in the early 1970s when Dutch manufacturer DAF was looking to add a larger, more modern car to its range. A partner was sought to help with the cost of developing the new model, and this led to Volvo buying a 35% stake in DAF's car division of DAF in 1972. Three years later Volvo increased their stake to 75%, thereby taking over the company.

In the meantime, work had been proceeding on the new car, the DAF 77. Styled by John De Vries (who later styled the Dutch-built Volvo 480), the 77 was to be a mid-sized hatchback with a 1.4 litre Renault engine and DAF's *Variomatic* continuously variable transmission.

As Volvo's influence grew, some alterations were made to the design, but its principal features, including its drivetrain, remained. One thing that did change, however, was its name: it was no longer to be launched as the DAF 77 but as the Volvo 343.

The 343 was only available with Variomatic until 1979, when a version with a manual gearbox was also offered. A five-door version, the 345, also joined the range that year. As time passed, further engine options were offered and the range was expanded to include a three-box saloon version.

In spite of its outmoded rear-wheel drive layout, the 300 series (of which the 343 was simply the lead-off model) sold fairly well and enjoyed a long production life, with the last of the 1.14 million cars built rolling out of the factory in 1991.

## G13

*In which year was a four-cylinder version of the Rover SD1 first offered for sale in the UK?*

**C.    1982**

The story of the Rover SD1 is very much a tale of what might have been.

At launch, the modern, attractive lines of the Rover SD1 made quite an impact with pundits and punters alike, if you'll excuse the vernacular. Furthermore, it was very attractively priced and its tried and trusted 3.5 litre V8 engine endowed it with the performance to match its looks.

But that, alas, was as good as things got for the SD1. Strikes hindered production from the get-go, one particularly unfortunate example being in 1977, when strike action resulted in a shortage of left-hand drive models at the very point when BL should have been cashing-in throughout Europe on the SD1's status as the newly-crowned European Car of the Year.

Later that year, six-cylinder versions of the SD1, the Rover 2300 and Rover 2600, were launched. These lower-priced but still capable models should have broadened its appeal, but problems with their underdeveloped engines sullied the SD1's reputation.

And then there was build quality, never British Leyland's strongest suit. Strikes, both at BL and their suppliers, had caused production to fall behind demand. This led to a rush to get cars to dealers, which in turn resulted in corners being cut in the quality control process, with obvious consequences.

Add in the 1979 energy crisis, consequent recession, BL's financial woes, yet more strikes and the 1981 mothballing of BL's Solihull factory, where the SD1 was built, and you might start to think that it never rained, only poured, where the SD1 was concerned.

Production shifted to Canley and a revised SD1 range was launched in 1982. The new range included a four-cylinder model, the Rover 2000, which used BL's 2.0 litre O-series engine. But although the introduction of the Rover 2000 meant BL could offer a cheaper, entry-level model, its performance was somewhat lacking.

Further models were added to the range, including a diesel, but the SD1 was now up against younger, fresher rivals. Demand fell sharply as the 1980s rolled on, and production finally ended in 1986.

**G14**

*Which manufacturer had an illuminated advertisement on the Eiffel Tower from 1925 to 1934?*

**B.    Citroën**

André Citroën knew a thing or two about promoting his company's products.

To mark the opening of the 1922 Paris Motor Show, an aircraft 'wrote' the word 'Citroën' in the sky over central Paris in letters that covered an area of around 5 kilometres. That was impressive enough, but Citroën really pulled out the stops three years later: they turned the Eiffel Tower into a nocturnal billboard.

In 1925, Paris played host to the International Exhibition of Modern Decorative and Industrial Arts. Running from April to October, the exhibition attracted millions of visitors from Europe and beyond. Recognising that no visit to Paris is complete without a sight-seeing trip to the Eiffel Tower, Citroën struck a deal whereby the Tower was fitted with 250,000 light bulbs and 370 miles of electrical wiring.

When night fell, a recurring animated light show would take place on three sides of the Tower, culminating in the word *Citroën* being displayed vertically between the second level and the observation deck, each letter being around 92 feet high.

The light show lasted until 1934, when Citroën's financial problems resulted in the display being switched off for good.

## G15

*Which company built the gas turbine engines that powered the prototype Advanced Passenger Train (APT-E) of the early 1970s?*

**B.     Rover**

The Advanced Passenger Train was a groundbreaking high-speed train that was designed to tilt when taking curves, thereby enabling them to be taken at a higher speed than achievable with a conventional train. In its initial form, its propulsion system was unusual too: each of its two power cars contained five gas turbine engines – four for motive power and the other for auxiliary power.

Great, you might think, but what's this doing in a book about cars? Well, the gas turbines used by the APT-E (as that first prototype was called) were built by Rover and derived from units designed for road use. Indeed, earlier versions of the Rover gas turbine powered both Rover's JET 1 experimental car in the 1950s and the Rover-BRM racing car which competed twice at Le Mans in the 1960s.

Sadly, the technology went nowhere in terms of both road and rail use. No gas turbine-powered car ever went into series production, and the APT-E gave way to the electrically-powered APT-P, with an inferior tilting mechanism, which briefly – and disastrously - entered service in the early 1980s.

## G16

*The first-generation VW Polo was beaten into production by which near-identical Audi model?*

**D.     Audi 50**

When is a VW Polo not a VW Polo? When it's an Audi 50.

In 1974, the Volkswagen Audi Group launched what was essentially the same car twice, six weeks apart.

First to arrive on the market was the Audi 50, a three-door hatchback with a transversely mounted petrol engine and front-wheel drive. This was followed just six weeks later by an almost identical car, the Volkswagen Polo.

The differences between the two were negligible: apart from the badging, the Audi 50 had a slightly more upmarket feel and was therefore a bit more expensive than the more basic Polo.

This price differential, plus the fact that the Polo range was expanded to offer a wider choice of engines and model specifications than its Audi cousin, meant that it was the more popular of the two with buyers. However, both models were sold side-by-side (albeit the Audi 50 never came to the UK) until 1978, whereupon the Audi 50 was dropped.

### G17

*Which one of the following Japanese cars **was** officially imported into the UK?*

**A.   Suzuki Cappuccino**

Since 1949, a special class of small vehicles has existed in Japan. Known as the *Kei* (a contraction of *Keijidosha,* or light automobile) class, these vehicles are built according to regulations that specify their size, engine capacity and power output. The regulations currently permit *Kei* class vehicles, which include both cars and minivans, to be no more than 3.4 metres long, have an engine capacity of no more than 660cc and a maximum power output of 63bhp.

*Kei* class vehicles have a lesser tax liability than larger vehicles and are subject to lower insurance premiums. Furthermore, their small dimensions and good fuel economy make them perfect for urban use.

They're hugely popular in Japan, and although the Japanese government significantly reduced their tax advantages in 2014, they still account for over 1/3$^{rd}$ of the Japanese new car market.

Minivans make up a large percentage of *Kei* car sales, but there have also been some excellent sports cars and coupés, such as the Honda Beat, Suzuki Cappuccino and Autozam AZ-1, which offer the style and driving pleasure of larger sports cars.

Neither the Beat nor the AZ-1 were officially imported to the UK, although some were privately imported. The Suzuki Cappuccino was, however, sold here between 1993 and 1995.

A two-seat roadster with a stowable hard top* instead of a fabric roof, the Cappuccino had a turbocharged 660cc engine delivering 63bhp, enough to take it from 0 to 60mph in 8.0 seconds and on to an electronically-limited top speed of 87mph.

Just over 1100 Cappuccinos were sold in the UK. As of the 2$^{nd}$ quarter of 2020, 187 were licensed with the DVLA and another 457 were SORNd.

For the avoidance of doubt, Nissan's Micra-based Figaro is not a *Kei* car nor was it sold in the UK by Nissan. However, around 4500 examples (out of 20,000 built) were brought into the UK by private importers.

* The Cappuccino's rear window and roll bar can be retracted into its bodyshell.

## G18

*What was the name of the electric car built by Scottish Aviation Limited that appeared on the 'Tomorrow's World' TV show in 1966?*

**A.     Scamp**

In the 1960s, Scottish Aviation Limited ('SAL'), an aircraft manufacturer based at Prestwick in Ayrshire, was looking at ways in which it might diversify its design and manufacturing operations.

One suggestion was the creation of an electric car that could be used for very short-range journeys such as, for example, that undertaken by a commuter from their home to a nearby railway station. SAL envisaged that such a car should be cheap to buy and run, be rechargeable using a domestic electricity supply (zero to full charge taking no more than 8 hours), have a maximum speed of 35mph, a range of around 25 miles and be simple to drive.

Designing the car was one thing; marketing it and setting up a retail network was quite another. However, the Electricity Council was interested in SAL's electric car and agreed that it could be sold in Electricity Board showrooms.

An experimental prototype was then constructed, tested and shown to the Electricity Council. This resulted in an order being placed for twelve cars so that staff from the Electricity Council and the various Electricity Boards could get hands-on experience of the car, now known as the Scamp.

A dozen Scamps were duly constructed, one of which appeared on the *Tomorrow's World* TV programme in 1966. But although it was praised by *Tomorrow's World* presenter Raymond Baxter, the reality was that much work needed to be done before the Scamp could be regarded as being fit for production. The suspension, in particular, was unsatisfactory, being apt to induce an unpleasant pitching motion on anything other than perfect road surfaces.

This was highlighted by tests conducted at the Motor Industry Research Association testing facility at the instance of the Electricity Council. To the surprise of SAL, they were to have no input into the test programme nor would their staff be able to observe the tests.

Unfortunately, the test results were little short of disastrous, with the Scamp's suspension faring particularly badly. No opportunity was afforded to SAL to address the problems and make the necessary modifications to the Scamp. Instead, the Electricity Council advised SAL that the Scamp was not fit for purpose and that, accordingly, they now sought to annul their earlier agreement.

Although the Scamp project team at SAL strongly believed that its issues were surmountable, the loss of its proposed retail network resulted in the cancellation of the project.

## G19

*Which of the following hatchbacks went into production first?*

**B.     Renault 16**

Launched in 1965, the Renault 16 wasn't the first hatchback to go into mass production but it was the most important.

Until the R16 came along, family cars were invariably of three box – engine bay, passenger cabin, and boot – configuration. This limited their practicality in terms of being able to carry larger or irregularly shaped items, that being the province of the estate car. However, the van-like appearance and increased length of estate cars wasn't to every buyer's liking, particularly if the extra load space on offer was only rarely going to be needed.

With the 16, Renault produced an intelligently designed car that was good to look at, offered much of the practicality of an estate car and was enjoyable to drive. It was voted European Car of the Year in 1966 and set a template for others to copy. Indeed, by the mid-1970s, hatchback cars had achieved significant success across several market sectors, and they would continue to increase in popularity for many years to come.

The Renault 16 continued in production until 1980, by which time a total of 1,845,959 had rolled out of the Renault factories.

## G20

*What do the Maserati Khamsin, VW Passat, Pagani Zonda and Austin Maestro have in common?*

**D.     They share their name with a wind**

Unlike the others, the Maestro is almost certainly not named after an air current but it nonetheless shares its name with a wind in the Adriatic Sea. In this respect it is the odd man out, as Volkswagen, Maserati and Pagani have each named several of their models after winds.

The Khamsin takes its name from a North African wind; the Passat's name comes from the German word, *Passatwinde,* which means Trade Winds; and the Zonda, launched in 1999, is named after a dry wind that occurs in the Argentinian Andes.

# It's a Numbers Game

## N1

*In 1994, there were 27,500 Renault 18s licensed with the DVLA. How many were licensed as at the 2nd quarter of 2020?*

**D.     23**

Produced in France between 1978 and 1986, the Renault 18 sold in reasonable numbers in the UK, making it onto the top 20 sales list in 1979, 1980 and 1981.

As with most cars of that era, the vast majority of R18s ended their days as cheap runabouts, to be used and discarded once the cost of keeping them on the road became too high relative to their value. Indeed, the DVLA data tells a sad tale of R18s being discarded by the thousands in the 1990s: between 1994 and 2000, the number of R18s licensed in the UK dropped from 27,500 to just 2494.

Which brings us to 2020 and the sad statistic that only 100 18s are known by the DVLA to exist in the UK. But although that overall number has remained more or less static in the last decade, the number of R18s licensed with the DVLA (as distinct from being on SORN) has gradually fallen, with only 23 having been licensed as at the 2nd quarter of 2020.

## N2

*How many Amphicars were built in its four year production run?*

**B.     3878**

The 1960s was a time of great innovation: humanity made its first journey into space and followed that up by visiting the moon; the prototype Concorde made its first flight; the ATM, pocket-sized calculator and barcode scanners were all born; and a German company put an amphibious car into production.

Available only as a convertible, the Amphicar was powered by a rear-mounted 1147cc four-cylinder Triumph engine (later versions could be had with 1296cc and 1493cc units) that gave it a maximum speed of around 70mph on land and 7 knots on water.

The Amphicar had two gear levers (one for road use, the other for on the water), two propellers, navigation lights, a bilge pump, and its doors were double-sealed. Steering was by means of its front wheels on both land and water.

It was sufficiently capable on water to be able to cross the English Channel under its own power. Indeed, one did so in 1965*. Using it on water, however, was apt to prove something of a chore, as thirteen separate points had to be greased when it returned to land.

Sales failed to meet its makers expectations and production ceased in 1965, although 'new' examples could still be purchased for some time thereafter.

The most famous Amphicar owner was Lyndon B. Johnson, the 36th President of the USA. Johnson took great delight in driving his Amphicar into the lake on his property in Texas without first telling his unsuspecting passengers that it was amphibious.

*Two Amphicars made the crossing in September 1965. When the engine of one became flooded due a blocked bilge pump, the other one successfully towed it to shore.

## N3

*When were the Type Approval Regulations introduced to the UK?*

**B.     1973**

One consequence of Britain's entry into the European Economic Community in 1973 was the requirement that EEC Directives be incorporated into UK law. Thus were the Type Approval Regulations born.

The first Motor Vehicle (Type Approval) Regulations were introduced by a Statutory Instrument in 1973. They came into effect on 10th August of that year but applied to new vehicles manufactured on or after 1st July. From that point on, no new vehicle could be sold in the UK unless it was certified as conforming with the Type Approval regulations*.

The Type Approval regulations thereafter became something of a moveable feast over the years, with additions and amendments being introduced by a series of Statutory Instruments.

*Very low-volume vehicle manufacturers can now apply for National Small Series Type Approval or Individual Vehicle Approval rather than go through the full EU-wide Type Approval process.

## N4

*How many examples of the first-generation Renault Espace were sold in its first month on sale?*

**A.    9**

At launch in 1984, the Renault Espace was unique, at least in Europe. It looked like a van, drove like a car and offered a multitude of different seat configurations to cater for a variety of human and non-human cargos. Oh, and its body was made of fibreglass. No wonder that it took car buyers a little while to catch on.

Just nine Espaces found buyers during its first month on sale, but sales gradually picked up: 2703 Espaces were sold in the second half of 1984, 14,248 in 1985, and 18,173 in 1986. By 1990, Renault was shifting almost 40,000 of them a year.

Second and third generation models followed, and by the late 1990s Matra Automobile (who had devised the Espace in the early 1980s*) was churning out just under 70,000 of them a year for Renault. However, Renault decided that they would manufacture the fourth generation Espace in-house. It was a decision that effectively, if unintentionally, sounded the death knell for Matra Automobile.

For a time, there was talk of MG Rover linking up with Matra

Automobile to produce a revised, Rover-powered version of the third generation Espace. The two companies were, however, unable to reach agreement and nothing came of the talks.

Renault continues to make the Espace, now in its fifth generation. But if you want one then you'll have to get used to left-hand drive: production of right-hand drive Espaces ended in 2012.

*The Espace has its origin in a concept dreamed up in the 1970s by Fergus Pollock, a British car designer who was then working for Chrysler Europe, with whom Matra had a strong commercial relationship.

## N5

*How many Morris Marinas were sold in the UK in its most successful year?*

**C.     115,041**

It has been the butt of many a joke and cruel prank, but the reality is that the Marina did pretty well for a car that was only ever meant to be a stop-gap model.

The Marina was never intended to be a clever design in the mould of some recent BLMC offerings. Instead, it was a simple, unpretentious car with conventional styling. It had rear-wheel drive, basic rear suspension and made use of the company's existing 1275cc A-series and 1798cc B-series engines.

Launched in 1971, it got off to a bad start, with around 30,000 cars being fitted with poorly set-up front suspension, which resulted in the 1.8 litre models, in particular, being prone to understeer of epic proportions. The problems were addressed but, even so, the Marina was never a sharp-handling car.

It was keenly priced, though, and this undoubtedly helped it record over 100,000 UK sales in both 1972 and 1973. The latter year was its most successful from a sales perspective, with 115,041 Marinas finding homes with UK buyers.

Sales thereafter dropped year on year, though the introduction in 1978 of a revised Marina with the new 1.7 litre O-series engine briefly turned the tide.

In 1980, the Marina was replaced by the Morris Ital, which was really little more than a Marina in a slightly different body. In this new guise, it soldiered on until it made way for the Austin Montego in 1984, a good 7 or 8 years after it ought to have been replaced.

Over 1.1 million Marinas were produced prior to its replacement by the Ital, of which over 700,000 were sold in the UK - not too shabby for a stop-gap model.

## N6

*What is the engine capacity of the Bugatti EB110 supercar?*

**C.     3500cc**

Back in the day the press rated the EB110 as the most user-friendly of supercars, one that could be driven to the local shops for a pint of milk without throwing a temper tantrum.

But make no mistake: the EB110 was a seriously fast and technologically innovative supercar. It had a carbonfibre chassis and permanent four-wheel drive; its 3500cc V12 engine was enhanced by four turbochargers; and its rear wing automatically raised and lowered depending on the speed at which it was travelling. That's impressive enough today, but in 1992 it was remarkable.

In standard form, the EB110 produced 533bhp, enough to propel it to a top speed of over 210mph. The Supersport model introduced in 1994 raised the bar further by offering an extra 70bhp in a package that weighed 200 kilogrammes less than the standard car. In the same year, Michael Schumacher took delivery of a yellow EB110 Supersport, being given a substantial discount on the price in recognition that his ownership of an EB110 would generate a lot of valuable publicity.

Unfortunately, Bugatti Automobili was weighed down by debts that it was unable to meet. It was declared bankrupt in September 1995, less than three years after the first production car was delivered. In that time, slightly fewer than 140 EB110s had been built. Following the closure of Bugatti, a handful of EB110s were completed by the German company, Dauer.

VW obtained the rights to use the Bugatti name in 1998 and has since produced the Veyron and Chiron hypercars. In 2021, Bugatti will release a car that pays tribute to the EB110, the Centodieci. Only ten Centodiecis will be made, but at a price of around 8 million Euros each, you could buy a fistful of EB110s and still have enough change to build a garage big enough – and grand enough – to keep them in.

## N7

*In what year did Chrysler sell their European car manufacturing operation to PSA (Peugeot Société Anonyme)?*

**A.    1978**

Unlike Ford and General Motors, Chrysler didn't have a significant presence in Europe until the 1960s. It attempted to rectify that by taking control of Simca in 1963 and Rootes in 1967.

In Rootes, it acquired some great marques (Humber and Sunbeam, in particular) but a somewhat uninspiring range of models. Much the same could be said of Simca's model range, save for the modern front-wheel drive 1100 hatchback that was launched in 1967.

With the benefit of hindsight, Chrysler ought to have made a much bigger effort to harmonise the efforts of its French and British arms and rationalise their model ranges. Instead, they each continued to plough separate furrows in terms of model development and component production. This led to a situation in which Simca increasingly concentrated on the development of front-wheel drive cars, and the former Rootes operation (now Chrysler United Kingdom) continued to build only rear-wheel drive vehicles.

In 1975, the UK government gave Chrysler UK significant financial assistance, part of which was to enable the company to build a new small car. Clearly, it would have made sense for the new car to follow the example of other European manufacturers and have front-wheel drive. Indeed, the components needed for it do so were readily available. These were, however, produced by Simca in France, and Chrysler could not be seen to be using UK taxpayers' money to safeguard jobs in France.

Ultimately, the new car, the Sunbeam, was built on a shortened Chrysler Avenger platform and used existing Chrysler UK mechanical components. This meant that it had rear-wheel drive, a configuration that led to it being less space-efficient than its front-wheel drive rivals. This translated into lost sales in a very competitive market sector.

By 1978, Chrysler UK was in dire straits. The Sunbeam was the only new car (albeit one with Avenger underpinnings) to have emerged from its factories since 1970. The rest of the UK-built Chryslers were old in both technology and appearance. Add in the other 1970s staples of rampant inflation and labour disputes and the picture was not a happy one.

To compound matters, Chrysler Europe's parent company was experiencing severe financial problems in the USA, and when Lee Iacocca became CEO in 1978 he decided that the company's European arm had to go. A deal with therefore struck with PSA whereby it took over Chrysler Europe lock, stock and accumulated debts for the princely sum of $1.

Neither of Chrysler Europe's British factories now exist: Linwood closed in 1981 and Ryton followed in 2006. Simca's Poissy plant remains in operation, however, and currently produces around 200,000 cars a year for Peugeot.

## N8

*In what year did Alfa Romeo's celebrated V6 Busso engine first appear in a production car?*

**C.    1979**

Designed by Giuseppe Busso, Alfa Romeo's wonderfully sonorous V6 engine first appeared in the Alfa 6 saloon in 1979.

In its initial guise, the V6 was a single overhead camshaft unit with two valves per cylinder, a displacement of 2492cc and an output of 156 bhp.

Over the years, the *Busso* (as it became known) acquired a second overhead camshaft and two extra valves per cylinder. It was produced in 2.0 litre (both with and without a turbocharger), 3.0 litre and, finally, 3.2 litre versions, and moved from a longitudinal to a transverse installation.

It performed sterling service in a wide variety of Alfa Romeos: the GTV 6, 75, 90, 147, 156, 164, 166, GT, GTV, Spider, SZ and RZ. It also popped up in the Fiat Croma and the Lancia Thema, Thetis and Kappa.

It was finally pensioned off in 2005 after twenty-six years in service.

## N9

*In which year did the Ford Fiesta first outsell the Mini in the UK?*

**B.    1980**

Ford was several years behind its European rivals when it came to including a small hatchback in its model range. Indeed, by the time that the Fiesta was launched in the UK in 1977, it faced established rivals from most of the main European manufacturers.

In the UK, however, Ford's biggest rival, British Leyland, did not build a small hatchback. Instead, the venerable Mini was all that they had to offer in the small car sector of the market.

Old though it was, the Mini was, however, still selling well in 1977. Well enough, in fact, to outsell the Fiesta in the UK until 1980, after which Mini sales fell away considerably, largely due to the introduction of BL's new Fiesta rival, the Austin Metro.

The Metro acquitted itself well at first, outselling the Fiesta in 1982 and 1983. However, the Metro became less competitive as time passed, a consequence of its manufacturer's inability to match the pace at which

Ford was able to revise and update the Fiesta.

## N10

*How long, to the nearest centimetre, was the 1981 Lincoln Town Car?*

**C.     557**

When we in the UK think of a 'town car', we invariably think of something small and highly manoeuvrable, such as an Austin Mini or a Smart Fortwo.

In the USA, however, 'town car' is another term for a limousine. So whilst people in the UK might have been surprised when Lincoln decided in 1981 that their new 5.57 metre (18 feet, 3 inches in old money) colossus should be called *Town Car*, it fitted the American definition of the term perfectly.

# General Knowledge III

## G21

*Which sports car manufacturer also produced an all-wheel drive pick-up in the 1980s?*

**C.    Lamborghini**

Given that the founder of Automobili Lamborghini, Ferrucio Lamborghini, was a son of the soil whose first major business was a company that manufactured tractors*, it seems logical that, of all the Italian supercar manufacturers, it was Lamborghini who would be the first to build a 4x4 pick-up. And that's how it panned out, with Lamborghini releasing the wonderfully barmy LM002 in 1986.

Its story begins in 1977 when, five years after being sold by its founder, Automobili Lamborghini was involved in the creation of the Cheetah, a four-wheel drive pick-up intended for military use.

The Cheetah project went no further than the production of a sole running prototype, but the idea of a Lamborghini pick-up was revived in the 1980s. The resulting LM002 of 1986 bore a strong resemblance to the Cheetah but was built around an entirely new chassis. Moreover, the front-engined LM002 used Lamborghini's own V12 engine rather than the Ford V8 found in the rear-engined Cheetah,

With a kerb weight of 2700 kilogrammes and the aerodynamics of a toilet block, the LM002 was never going to be blisteringly fast, even with over 440 bhp on tap. Its off-road ability was, however, very impressive, thanks to its high ground clearance, locking differentials, specially designed Pirelli Scorpion run-flat tyres and abundant torque.

The LM002 was sold between 1986 and 1993. Sources differ as regards the exact number produced, but the consensus is that it was over 300. Many still remain today, but don't be expecting a bargain: with prices starting at around £220,000, a 30 year old LM 002 costs more to buy than a brand new Lamborghini Urus.

*Lamborghini Trattoria was founded by Ferrucio Lamborghini in 1948 and has continued to build tractors right up to the present day.

## G22

*The Hillman Hunter was built in Iran until 2005 under what name?*

**C.     Paykan**

Introduced in 1966, the Hillman Hunter was a member of the Rootes Arrow family of badge-engineered saloons, estates, coupés and pick-ups.

Aside from the Hunter, other members of the Arrow clan included the Humber Sceptre, Hillman Minx, Singer Gazelle, Sunbeam Rapier and Hillman Hustler.

Following the acquisition by Chrysler of a majority share in the Rootes Group in 1967, the Hunter eventually became the only version of the Arrow offered in the UK. It retained the Hillman name until September 1977, when it became a Chrysler.

The Hunter was sold in Iran, where it was known as the Paykan, from 1966. At first, the Paykan was assembled in Iran from Complete Knock Down kits supplied from Europe, but the production tooling was moved to Iran after the Hunter ceased to be built in Europe.

The Paykan saloon continued to be built until 2005, but a pick-up version, the Bardo, continued in production for a further ten years.

## G23

*What was the first Japanese car to be officially imported to the UK?*

**A.     Daihatsu Compagno**

Unless you're a real devotee of Japanese cars, it's unlikely that you'll have heard of the Daihatsu Compagno.

The first four-wheel Daihatsu car, the Vignale-styled Campagnola was introduced in its home market in 1963, initially in saloon and estate form. The first versions were powered by a 797cc petrol engine, but a 958cc version of the saloon appeared in 1965 along with pick-up and convertible versions.

Daihatsu was keen to establish a presence in Europe, and in 1965 it commenced exports of the Compagno to the UK. The Compagno failed, however, to win over the British car buying public, causing Daihatsu to leave the UK market for a time.

After its re-entry to the UK in the 1970s, the marque enjoyed a modest measure of success with a string of models, including the Charade, Appluase, Fourtrak and Sportrak.

## G24

*Which company manufactured Rostyle wheels in the UK?*

**C.  Rubery Owen**

Rostyle pressed-steel wheels originated in the USA in the 1960s, where they were known as the 'Magnum 500' and often fitted to muscle cars. They were no less popular in the UK, where they could be found on a wide variety of cars - from the humble Mini to the classy Jensen Interceptor - as an alternative to alloy wheels. They were last offered as a manufacturer-fitted wheel in the 1990s.

As with many iconic product names, *Rostyle* has a very simple origin, being a portmanteau of R(ubery) O(wen) style.  And, at least in my opinion, *Rostyle* sounds far better than *Magnum 500*.

## G25

*Which Mitsubishi-owned Australian marque sold a badge-engineered Mitsubishi Sigma in the UK between 1982 and 1984?*

**D.  Lonsdale**

Back in the 1980s, a voluntary agreement limited the importation of

Japanese-made cars to the UK to an annual figure not exceeding 11% of the total number of of new cars sold in the UK.

Mitsubishi attempted to get around this restriction by importing cars to the UK from its production facilities in Australia. In order to facilitate this, it created a new marque, Lonsdale, which took its name from the suburb in Adelaide in which Mitsubishi had an engine plant.

Only one Lonsdale model was offered in the UK, the Mitsubishi Sigma-based YD. Mitsubishi hoped to import 5,000 Lonsdales a year but sales were so poor that the venture was abandoned after only two years. All remaining unsold Lonsdales in the UK were then rebadged and sold as Mitsubishi Galants (the Galant and the Sigma being the same car).

In spite of the poor sales figures and the passage of time since the venture ceased, a few Londsdales have survived in the UK: as at the second quarter of 2020, 3 were licensed and a further 2 were on SORN.

### G26

*The 'MR' in the name of the Toyota MR2 is an abbreviation of..?*

**C.**     **Midship Runabout**

Launched in 1984, it's fair to say that the first-generation Toyota MR2 was more than just a runabout. A lot more.

The result of a project that commenced in the mid-1970s, the MR2 was launched in 1984, with UK sales commencing the following year.

In European form, the MR2* came with a 1587cc fuel-injected engine that featured double overhead camshafts and four valves per cylinder. Power output was 120 bhp, enough to take the MR2 to a top speed of 120 mph and cover the 0 to 60 mph sprint in 7.7 seconds. It stopped, steered and handled well, too, offering a little taste of supercar motoring at an affordable price. The motoring press and the public both loved it, and rightly so.

Two further generations followed, in 1990 and 1999 respectively, but neither was quite able to match the impact made by the original. Production ended in 2007.

* The MR2 was known as the 'MR' in France. As to the reason why, let's just say that the French pronunciation of 'MR2' is uncomfortably close to a word that is considered offensive in la République.

## G27

*Ferrari and Dodge have each produced a model with which name?*

### A.    Daytona

Okay, I admit it: the Ferrari Daytona was never actually called that by the company itself (to them, it's the 365 GTB/4 and 365 GTS/4) but pretty much everyone refers to it by that name. And custom trumps formality, doesn't it?

The Dodge, on the other hand, was actually badged 'Daytona'. But if you're thinking that it was named after the Ferrari then you'd be wrong: it took its name from the Dodge Charger Daytona* that raced in NASCAR at the tail end of the 1960s and was built in limited numbers for the road.

Apart from both cars being front-engined coupés (the Ferrari was also produced in convertible form), they had little in common. The Ferrari was powered by a 4.4 litre V12 engine that drove the rear wheels; the Dodge mostly made do with four-cylinder engines (a 3.0 litre V6 version was introduced in 1990) that powered the front wheels. Needless to say, the Ferrari was very much the quicker of the two, as well as being much more expensive than its Dodge namesake.

That disparity in price remains, to the extent that in 2020 you could pick up a couple of dozen Dodge Daytonas and a modest condo in Santa Cruz for the price of a single Ferrari Daytona.

That's not to say, of course, that the Dodge is a bad car. It isn't. Indeed, the Turbo version was good enough to make *Road and Track's* top ten list in 1984. Moreover, it sold well enough in the USA to warrant a nine year production run during which it was restyled twice.

\* Dodge has revived the Daytona name from time to time, usually as a specific model in its Charger range.

## G29

*How many cars did Lotus build in 1981?*

**B.     345**

The late 1970s and early 1980s was a time of great economic strife which, at least in part, was the result of the second great energy crisis to have struck within six years.

For Lotus, the result of this economic downturn was a sharp reduction in demand for their products. This led to a significant fall in production from 1200 cars in 1978 to just 345, all but 44 of which were Esprits, in 1981.

Although production increased in 1982, it did not approach 1978 levels until 1988, when 1302 cars were built. The introduction of the new Elan M100 in late 1989 saw annual production exceed 2000 cars in both 1990 and 1991, but another recession in the early 1990s saw sales slump once more, with the result that production of both the M100 and the Excel ceased in 1992\*.

\*The M100 made a comeback in 1994 as a limited edition model to use up Lotus's stockpile of engines and gearboxes.

## G30

*Which production car of the late 1980s and early 1990s had retractable doors?*

**B.     BMW Z1**

It's fair, I think, to say that BMW isn't exactly renowned for producing left-field cars. Instead, they stick largely to the straight and narrow when it comes to car design. And that's a pity as, if the Z1 is anything to go by, they're more than capable of producing offbeat cars that excel.

Designed by Harm Lagaay, the Z1 cheerfully threw the BMW design manual out with the bathwater. Its exterior was made up of detachable thermoplastic and fibreglass panels which could, said BMW, be removed in around 40 minutes. In reality, it took rather longer than that, but no matter; what really counted was the fact that you could completely change the colour of a Z1 just by swapping over body panels. Indeed, BMW envisaged that some owners would buy a spare set of panels so that they could do just that.

The real showstopper was not, however, the panels but the doors. These didn't open in the conventional sense; in fact they didn't open at all. Instead, they retracted into the sills. And what's more, the Z1 could be driven with its doors down.

But the Z1 wasn't all about its doors and interchangeable panels: it was the first BMW to use the company's Z-axle multi-link suspension; motive power was courtesy of a creamily smooth 2.5 litre straight six; it looked great, particularly with the hood down; and its chassis was made of hot-dip galvanised steel.

The Z1 was produced between 1989 and 1991, but although officially imported to the UK it was only available in left-hand-drive form.

## G30

*From what did the Matra M530 take its name?*

**A.     A guided missile**

Mecanique Aviation Traction was founded in 1945 by Marcel Chassagny. For the first two decades of its existence, the company operated principally in the aerospace and defence sectors, but in 1964 it purchased Automobiles René Bonnet, a small, specialist car manufacturer.

A new subsidiary of Matra was formed, Matra Sports. In this guise, Matra resumed production of the Bonnet Djet, changing its name first to Matra-Bonnet Djet and finally to Matra Jet. Matra Sports also went racing, winning championships in Formulas 3, 2 and 1, and taking a hat-trick of wins in the Le Mans 24 Hours.

In 1967, Matra launched a new road car, the first to have been designed in-house. Named after one of the company's air-to-air guided missiles, the R.530, the M530 was a mid-engined 2+2 seat sports car powered by a 1.7 litre Ford V4 engine. It had an advanced specification for its time, including disc brakes all round, pop-up headlamps and (on most models) a detachable, longitudinally-split targa roof.

In all, 9609 M530s were built before it gave way on the production lines to another innovative sports car, the three-seat Matra-Simca Bagheera.

# *Motorsport*

## M1

*In which car did Andrew Cowan win the 1968 London-Sydney Marathon?*

**A.     Hillman Hunter**

The concept of a rally that would run from London to Sydney was conceived in late 1967 during a lunchtime discussion between Max Aitken, the proprietor of the Daily Express newspaper, and two of the paper's executives, Jocelyn Stevens and Tommy Sopwith.

At the time there was much concern about the UK government's decision to devalue the pound by 14%, thus reducing the exchange rate with the US dollar from $2.40 to the pound to $1.80. This followed a period of domestic and international strife that included the 1967 Six-Day War between Israel and Egypt, Syria and Jordan; the closure of the Suez Canal and consequent rise in the price of oil and other commodities; France's refusal to agree to the United Kingdom's application to become a member of the EEC; and damaging strikes by dock and railway workers.

The idea behind that the rally was that it would help to boost morale, act as a showcase for British engineering and, hopefully, boost export sales of British-made cars.

The Express put up a prize of £10,000 to whomever won the rally, to which The Daily Telegraph added further cash prizes. With the two newspapers at the helm, the rally's formal title became the *Daily Express-Daily Telegraph London-Sydney Marathon.*

Following the start of the rally in London, the competitors drove to Dover, where they took the ferry to Calais. The route then took them to Paris, Turin, Belgrade and Istanbul, where they crossed the Bosporus by ferry before heading on to Teheran, Kabul, Sarobi, Delhi and Bombay (Mumbai).

From Bombay, the remaining competitors were transported by ship to Fremantle in western Australia. They then headed east across Australia to the finishing line in Sydney. All told, the rally lasted 23 days and covered a distance of just over 10,000 miles.

Roger Clark led for much of the way in his Ford Cortina Lotus, but a series of mechanical issues in Australia put paid to his hopes. This left Lucien Bianchi in the lead but his rally ended with under 100 miles to run when his Citroën DS had a head-on collision with a motorist who had strayed onto the closed road being used by the rally. Paddy Hopkirk, then running third, stopped to render assistance to the injured occupants of the cars. The next competitor on the scene, second-placed Andrew Cowan, also stopped but was waved through as the situation was being dealt with.

The result was that Cowan (with co-drivers Colin Malkin and Brian Coyle) won the rally in a Hillman Hunter, with Hopkirk's BMC 1800 in second place and Australia's Ian Vaughan third in his Ford XT Falcon GT. Long-time leader Roger Clark finished the rally in ninth place.

Cowan repeated his 1968 victory when the rally was next run in 1977. It has since returned in 1993, 2000, 2004 and 2014.

For Cowan, his 1968 victory was one of several he took in long-distance rallies. He later went on to head Mitsubishi Ralliart Europe, for whom Tommi Makinen took four consecutive (1996 to 1999) World Rally Championships.

## M2

*Which future F1 world champion raced in a round of the Volkswagen-organised Scirocco Junior Cup in 1976?*

**C.     Keke Rosberg**

The first-generation VW Scirocco was a handsome, well-crafted coupé with good road manners and a reasonable price tag. Indeed, its early versions wanted for little, save perhaps for a bit more power.

It got that in 1976 with the arrival of the 1.6 litre fuel-injected GTI model. With 110 bhp on tap (25 more than the 1.5 litre version could offer), it turned a good car into a great one.

That being so, you might think that the Scirocco Junior Cup racing series was a clever marketing ploy intended to show off the Scirocco's new-found pace. But although it may ultimately have had that effect, it was launched several months before the Scirocco GTI appeared. Moreover, the cars that took part in it did not wear GTI badging even though they were equipped with the same fuel-injected 1588cc engine as it.

The Scirocco Junior Cup was open to prospective racers under the age of 30. Around 1200 people expressed an interest in competing, but this number fell to 200 after a deposit of 5000 Deutschmarks was sought. The remaining applicants were then invited to attend a test session. The best 45 were selected to enter the championship, although their participation was contingent on them purchasing a specially prepared Scirocco from VW, albeit at less than cost price. Five other cars were prepared by VW for use by guest drivers.

The series was comprised of eight rounds, three of which were held at Hockenheim. The guest drivers included Keke Rosberg, the reigning German Formula Super Vee champion, who took part in the second race of the series, held on the island of Sylt, but failed to finish in the top ten.

Four of the eight races were won by Manfred Winkelhock but this wasn't enough to secure the championship. Even so, it was the first step of a career that took him to F1, where he once again encountered Keke Rosberg. Winkelhock started 47 Grands Prix but seldom had a car capable of finishing in a points-scoring position. Rosberg, on the other hand, did rather better in F1 than he had at the wheel of a Scirocco, winning five Grands Prix and the 1982 World Drivers' Championship.

The sons of both men also raced in F1. For Markus Winkelhock, his F1 career amounted to a single race. Nico Rosberg enjoyed a rather longer and more successful career in F1, competing for eleven full seasons and emulating his father by winning the World Drivers' Championship.

## M3

*In what country did the Renault 12 win a round of the World Rally Championship?*

**A.     USA**

Yes, you read that right: the USA played host to a round of the World

Rally Championship ('WRC') in the early 1970s. In fact, the aptly named Press-on-Regardless Rally formed part of the WRC calendar in the first two years of the championship's existence.

In its early days, the Press-on-Regardless Rally was a regularity rally, in which the challenge was to complete stages in a specific time rather than as quickly as possible. Its format changed in 1969, when it became a stage rally – i.e. one in which the objective is to complete a stage in the lowest possible time. It made its international debut in this new form in 1972, when it formed part of the International Championship for Manufacturers, the predecessor of the World Rally Championship.

When the WRC started in 1973, the Press-on-Regardless was included in its schedule. The competition was thin in that first year, with many of the European teams not making the trip to the USA. The field for the Detroit-based event was stronger in 1974, however, with Sandro Munari, Simo Lampinen, Bernard Darniche, Jean-Pierre Nicolas, Markku Alén and Jean-Luc Therier all taking part.

Victory went to Therier and co-driver Christian Delferier in their Renault 17 Gordini, with Alén second in his Fiat 124 Abarth and Nicolas third in another 17 TS.

It was the only WRC win for the Renault 17, the penultimate WRC win for Therier, and the Press-on-Regardless Rally's final appearance in the World Rally Championship. Indeed, it would be 12 years before the USA again hosted a round of the championship.

## M4

*Finland's Pauli Toivonen controversially won the 1966 Monte Carlo Rally in which car?*

### C.     Citroën DS 21

In 1966, the Mini Coopers of Timo Makinen, Rauno Aaltonen and Paddy Hopkirk took a clean sweep of the podium positions in the Monte Carlo Rally. Until, that is, the stewards disqualified them on the basis that their headlamps did not conform to the regulations. Fifty-plus years on, it remains a hugely controversial decision.

Having won the event with Hopkirk in 1964 and Makinen in 1965, BMC was confident of further success in 1966. However, new regulations had been introduced for that year, in terms of which cars competing in Group 1, such as the Mini Cooper, had to be fitted with a number of production standard components, including the engine and wheels. However, the first draft of the regulations permitted a free choice of lights, both in terms of their number and specification. That draft was subsequently replaced by a second version, in which a free choice of lights was not permitted.

Unfortunately, neither the British-based teams nor the Royal Automobile Club, which was responsible for scrutineering the cars departing from London, was made aware of the second version of the regulations. Consequently, a number of British-based competitors, including the BMC Mini Coopers and the Ford Cortina Lotus of Roger Clark, had exercised what they believed was their right to a free choice of lights.

The problems started in France, where several privately-entered British crews were disqualified due to their cars having too many lights. However, none of the cars in Group 1 were disqualified even though their lights obviously failed to comply with the regulations. Indeed, they were allowed to continue to the end of the rally, which is when all hell broke loose.

When the rally ended in Monte Carlo, there was much to celebrate for the British teams: the trio of Minis filled the top three places, Roger Clark had brought home his Cortina in fourth and Rosemary Smith had finished sixth overall and won the Coupe des Dames. And then the scrutineers descended upon them. The Minis in particular were subjected to a detailed inspection, and when that failed to yield anything that could be used against them, attention was turned to the lights.

The issue was that the Minis had been fitted with single-filament bulbs instead of the double-filament items used on production cars. This meant that the headlamp beams were not capable of being dipped; instead, the lights were dipped by switching from the headlamps to the spotlamps. More pertinently, however, this meant that the lights were technically illegal, at least in terms of the second version of the regulations.

The three Minis, Clark and Smith were all disqualified, some eighteen hours after the rally ended and three days after the scrutineers in France had allowed them to continue in spite of the illegality of their lights.

Finland's Pauli Toivonen was therefore declared the winner, having finished fifth on the road in his Citroën DS. Toivonen, who scored several major wins in his rallying career and won the 1968 European Rally Championship, was unimpressed and somewhat embarrassed at being handed a win that he had not earned. When his son, Henri Toivonen, took a dominant win in the 1986 Monte Carlo Rally, Pauli's comment was simple, succinct and heartfelt: "Now the name of Toivonen has been cleared."

**M5**

*In 1980 and 1981, which car did Stirling Moss drive in the British Saloon Car Championship?*

**B.    Audi 80 GLE**

Stirling Moss was in his prime when he suffered serious injuries in a race at Goodwood in 1962. A year later, his physical injuries having healed, Moss tested a Lotus 19 sports car at Goodwood. Although his lap times were good, Moss felt that he was no longer able to drive the car instinctively. Consequently, he decided to retire from motor racing.

It was a decision that he came to regret, for at the time of the Goodwood test he had not recovered from the psychological effects of his accident. Had he waited for a few more months then it is likely that he would have felt able to resume his racing career.

In the years that followed, he participated in an occasional race, but in 1980 came the surprise, but welcome, announcement that he was making a full-time return to racing with Audi in what was then the British Saloon Car Championship.

Moss competed for two years in the championship, partnering Richard Lloyd in 1980 and Martin Brundle in 1981. But although his return made for great box office, results were disappointing. Moss did not return to the championship after 1981 and thereafter competed mostly in historic motor racing until he finally hung up his crash helmet in 2011.

## M6

Bernard Unett won the British Saloon Car Championship three times at the wheel of which car?

**A.    Hillman/Chrysler Avenger**

From its inception in 1958 until 1990, the British Saloon Car Championship (it became the British Touring Car Championship in 1987) operated on a system under which each car competed in one of four classes defined by engine size.

This meant that entrants not only competed for overall race positions but also against other cars in their class. Points were awarded according to where each driver finished in his or her class rather than their overall race position. At the end of the season, the championship was awarded to the driver who had scored the most points in his or her class.

The result of this was that the winner of the championship usually came from one of the one of the smaller-engined classes rather than the 'top' class for cars with the largest engines. The reason for this was that the top class was usually the most competitive, thus making it harder for one driver to dominate. Indeed, in the thirty-three seasons to 1990, the championship was only won five times by a driver competing in the class for cars with the largest capacity engines.

Bernard Unett's three title wins came in 1974, 1976 and 1977, all at the wheel of an Avenger: a 1.5 litre model in 1974, and a 1.3 litre in 1976 and 1977. In 1976, he won his class in all nine of the championship rounds.

In 1991, the championship was changed to a single class, with the maximum engine capacity set at 2.0 litres. It has retained that formula ever since, although a separate Production class did feature from 2000 to 2003 as a way of helping to augment the field following the withdrawal of several of the manufacturers' teams.

## M7

*A Group B version of which of these cars was produced?*

**B.   Citroën BX**

Telling the story of Group B would fill a book on its own, so what follows is an ultra-condensed version.

Group B was a set of regulations created by motorsport's governing body, the FIA, which covered sports car racing and rallying. Cars built to Group B regulations had two things in common: they were very powerful and very quick.

The Group B regulations came into force in 1982 and led to some of the wildest rally cars ever, such as the Lancia 037, Lancia Delta S4, Audi Quattro S4, Peugeot 205 T16, Ford RS200 and Metro 6R4.

As manufacturers were obliged to build at least 200 roadgoing examples of Group B cars for homologation purposes, people with sufficient money and inclination could buy a road-legal version of a Group B car.

The Group B era didn't last long. The problem was that the rally cars, in particular, were just too fast, too powerful (the Delta S4 had a turbocharger and a supercharger and, in rally trim, could pump out over 500 bhp) and too dangerous.

Two disasters in 1986 spelled the end for Group B. In the Rally Portugal, a Ford RS200 slid into a group of spectators, killing three people, and in the Tour De Corse, the Delta S4 of Henri Toivonen and Sergio Crespo left the road, plunged down a hillside and exploded, killing both men. This led to the FIA banning Group B cars from the World Rally Championship after the end of the season.

But although it was short-lived, Group B had caught the imagination of a number of manufacturers, including Alfa Romeo, Audi, Ferrari, Peugeot and Lancia. Citroën also got in on the act and created a Group B version of the BX: the BX 4TC.

The BX 4TC Evolution contested the opening three rounds of the 1986 World Rally Championship. Alas, it was both overweight and underpowered in comparison to the competition. And although Jean-Claude Andruet brought his 4TC home sixth in the Swedish Rally, it simply wasn't competitive against its more highly-developed competition. Citroën therefore pulled the plug on the project, buying back and scrapping many of the roadgoing versions of the 4TC as well as most of the Evolution versions used in rallying.

Neither VW nor BMW produced a dedicated Group B version of any of their cars, although the BMW M1 was classified as a Group B car in sports car racing, and another M1 was converted to Group B spec. for rallying.

Lotus did not produce a Group B version of any of their cars, but was, however, involved in the creation of a Talbot Horizon Group B prototype. Armed with a mid-mounted 2.2 litre Lotus engine, the Horizon would have probably have replaced the Sunbeam Lotus as Talbot's World Rally Championship contender but for the advent of the Audi Quattro.

Realising that four-wheel drive was now an essential ingredient for WRC success, Peugeot Talbot cancelled the Horizon project and started afresh. The result was the Peugeot 205 T16, which the World Rally Championship (Drivers and Constructors) in 1985 and 1986.

As for the Horizon project, two prototypes were built, one with a normally aspirated Lotus 2174cc engine and the other with a turbocharged version of the unit.

## M8

*The last two-wheel drive car to win the World Rally Championship was the...?*

**C.     Lancia 037**

There's no question that the Audi Quattro revolutionised rallying. However, the Lancia 037 managed, for one glorious season, to take the fight to the Quattro and emerge triumphant.

The 037 was Lancia's first attempt at a Group B car. Very loosely based on the Montecarlo coupé (the centre section was the same), it was powered by a mid-mounted, supercharged 2.0 litre engine (later increased to 2.1 litres). It was low, light (its kerb weight was under a tonne) and only ever made in rear-wheel drive form.

It first competed in 1982 but really came into its own the following year, when Walter Rohrl and Markku Alén won five rallies between them and Lancia beat Audi to the Constructors' title.

Pickings were slimmer in 1984 as the 037 faced an uphill battle against not only the Audi Quattro but also Peugeot's new 205 T16. The 037 was, however, wheeled out for one last campaign in 1985. In a season marred by tragedy - Attilio Bettega was fatally injured after crashing his 037 in the Tour De Corse – the 037 failed to finish higher than third in a WRC rally.

It was replaced for the final round of the 1985 season by Lancia's new Group B challenger, the four-wheel drive Delta S4. Henri Toivonen gave the Delta a spectacular debut by taking it to victory in the Lombard RAC Rally, with team-mate Alén coming home second.

One final thing: in the 1983 Monte Carlo Rally, the works 037s made mid-stage stops to receive new tyres from waiting service crews. Each tyre stop took around a minute but saved time overall. Indeed, along with Lancia's imaginative decision to deposit around 300 tonnes of salt on the rally's special stages (to melt the snow and thereby negate the advantage enjoyed by the Audi Quattro), the tyre stops helped the 037s to finish the rally in first and second places.

Lancia thereafter continued to use pit stops in rallies for several years.

## M9

*Which of the following cars did **not** win a World Rally Constructors' Championship?*

**B.** **Opel Ascona 400**

Here's a curious thing: although the World Rally Championship was inaugurated in 1973, there was no Drivers' Championship until 1977, and even then it was referred to as the FIA Cup for Drivers for the first two years.

But I digress. The early years of the world championship were dominated by Italian cars, with Lancia taking three successive championships with the Stratos and Fiat following that with two titles for the 131 Abarth.

Remarkable as it may seem to those who followed rallying in the 1970s, Ford scored just one win in the Constructors' Championship, with the Escort RS1800 taking in 1979.

Come the 1980s, the Opel Ascona 400, very much a staple of the World Rally Championship, found itself up against the might of the Audi Quattro. Opel never won the Constructors' Championship but Walter Rohrl's brilliance at the wheel of his Ascona 400 took him to the Drivers' Championship in 1982, beating the works Audi drivers, Michele Mouton and Hannu Mikkola.

Which brings us to the Talbot Sunbeam Lotus. In its debut season in 1980, Henri Toivonen took it to victory in the RAC Rally, thus becoming the youngest-ever winner of a world championship rally. It did even better in 1981, winning the Constructors' World Championship for the Talbot team and taking Guy Frequelin and Jean Todt (yes, *that* Jean Todt) to second in the Drivers' Championship.

**M10**

*In which car did Paul Newman win the first of his four SCCA championships?*

**A.    Triumph TR6**

Like Steve McQueen, his co-star in the 1974 disaster movie *'The Towering Inferno'*, Paul Newman had a taste for motorsport. But whereas McQueen mostly competed off-road on two wheels, Newman's preference was for circuit racing on four.

Newman's latent passion for racing was ignited when he took a driving course at the Watkin's Glen circuit in preparation for his role in the 1969 film, *'Winning'*. Three years later, he entered his first professional motor race at Thompson International Speedway, Connecticut.

The following year, 1973, he drove a Nissan 510 in the Sports Car Club of America national finals, finishing ninth in his class. He improved to sixth in his class in 1975, but his breakthrough came in 1976 when took his Nissan 510 to third in the B Sedan class before winning the D Production class in a Triumph TR6.

He won the C Production class in 1979 in a Nissan 280ZX. That same year, he co-drove a Porsche 935 with Klaus Ludwig and Dick Barbour in the Le Mans 24 Hours, the trio finishing second overall.

Newman took two further wins in the SCCA National Championships, winning the GT1 category in both 1985 and 1986 at the wheel of a Nissan 280ZX. He kept racing into his 80s, reportedly winning a race at Lime Rock at the age of 81.

He also became a team owner, co-founding with Carl Haas the Newman/Haas team that won 8 ChampCar championships, including the 1993 championship with Nigel Mansell.

# General Knowledge IV

### G31

*What was the first water-cooled Volkswagen production car?*

**D.     K70**

The first water-cooled Volkswagen was actually an NSU.

NSU (an abbreviation of 'Neckarsulm', the German town where it was based) started out in 1873 as a manufacturer of knitting machines. The company was originally based in Riedlingen and known as *Mechanische Werkstätte zur Herstellung von Strickmaschinen.* It moved to Neckarsulm a few years later, changed its name to *Neckarsulmer Strickmaschinen-Fabrik AG* and thereafter diversified into bicycle manufacturing. The company started to use NSU as a brand name around this time, retaining it when they moved into motorcycle and car production in the early part of the 20<sup>th</sup> century.

In 1964, NSU was the first European manufacturer to offer a rotary-engined car, the NSU Spider. A more ambitious programme followed, with the company joining forces with Citroën in 1967 to create Comotor, a Luxembourg-based company specialising in the design and manufacture of rotary engines. That year also saw NSU launch their sophisticated new saloon, the Ro80.

Styled by Claus Luthe, the Ro80 was a remarkable car for its time. Underneath its glassy, aerodynamic body lay a twin-rotor engine that drove the front wheels via a semi-automatic gearbox. In addition, it was equipped with disc brakes all round, a rarity at the time, with the front brakes being mounted inboard. Unsurprisingly, it was voted European Car of the Year in 1968.

But then it all started to go wrong for NSU. The Ro80's engine suffered serious reliability issues, mostly arising from premature wear of the rotor tip seals. Moreover, the Ro80's fuel economy was poor (a common feature of rotary engines) and this, plus the reliability issues, meant that sales were much lower than anticipated. Add in the cost of setting up Comotor and the result was that NSU found itself in a perilous financial position as the end of the decade approached.

In the meantime, the company had been working on a new, conventionally-powered car: the K70. Intended to slot into the NSU range below the Ro80, the K70 featured a 1.6 litre water-cooled engine that powered the front wheels. It was scheduled for launch in 1969, and saloon and estate versions were to be offered.

And then VW stepped in. The VW that existed at the tail end of the 1960s was a far cry from the company we know today. Its model range, which consisted entirely of rear-engined, air-cooled cars, was in need of modernisation. Taking over NSU, and thereby acquiring the modern, production-ready K70, therefore made a great deal of sense.

VW's takeover of NSU, which was presented as a merger, went ahead in 1969. When the K70 entered production the following year, it wore a VW badge and was built at Volkswagen's Salzgitter factory. It was offered only in saloon form; the estate version never appeared.

With around 210,000 examples being built over its five year production run, the K70 wasn't a roaring success in terms of sales, but it pointed the way ahead for Volkswagen; within half a decade the company had released a series of seminal water-cooled, front-wheel drive models, including the Golf, Polo and Scirocco.

### G32

*What was unusual about the Rover T4 prototype of 1961?*

**B. It had a gas turbine engine**

The rotary engine wasn't the only blind alley into which motor manufacturers ploughed resources in the 1960s.

Gas turbine engines are, like rotary engines, renowned for their smoothness. Moreover, they are lighter, have better power to weight ratios than piston engines, and can run on a wide variety of liquid propellants – Chrysler said that their Turbine Car of the 1960s could run on anything from peanut oil to perfume.

But as in the case of rotary engines, gas turbines were not fuel-efficient. And that wasn't the only issue: they generated a lot of heat, produced a lot of nitrogen oxide, and had poor throttle response, no engine braking and a lack of flexibility.

These issues did not, however, prevent manufactures from exploring the technology. Rover was an early adopter of it, at least in terms of prototype vehicles. The first and most celebrated of these was JET 1, an open-top two-seater built around a modified Rover P4 platform. Unveiled in 1950, JET 1 was gradually developed until, in 1952, it covered the flying kilometre at Jabbeke in Belgium at an average speed of 152 mph.

The company also went racing with a gas turbine engine, competing in the 1963 and 1965 Le Mans 24 Hours in partnership with BRM. The Rover-BRM car was never in contention for victory but performed respectably, making it to the finish on both occasions.

In terms of road cars, however, the pinnacle of Rover's achievements was the T4. Based on the prototype P6 saloon, the T4's gas turbine engine drove the front wheels. First shown in 1961, two years before the P6 went into production, the T4 was fast and had improved fuel consumption (in the region of 20 miles per gallon) over earlier gas turbine prototypes. Rover toyed with the idea of offering it as a production model, but its anticipated price tag of around £4000 would have made it more expensive than many houses.

Having decided not to commercialise the T4, Rover did not build any further gas turbine-powered cars. Many of their previous efforts were, however, preserved for posterity, and both the T4 and the Rover-BRM racing car can be seen at the British Motor Museum in Warwickshire.

## G33

*The Renault 7, a booted version of the Renault 5 hatchback, was built and (mostly) sold in which country?*

**B.     Spain**

Saloons based on hatchbacks are apt to be a curious-looking lot.

The Renault 7 is no exception to this; it would have looked ungainly even had its boot not sat lower than its bonnet. Somebody must have liked it though, as it stayed in production for a decade and found homes with over 159,000 buyers.

A product of Renault's Spanish subsidiary, FASA-Renault, the 7 (originally called the *Seite)* was launched in 1974. Offered only in four-door form*, the 7 had a slightly larger wheelbase than its hatchback sibling and came with chrome bumpers rather than the plastic, impact-absorbing items fitted to the 5. Another point of difference lay in the motive power department, the 7 only being offered with a 1037cc engine.

A restyled version was launched in 1979, at which time the 1037cc engine was replaced by an 1108cc unit. Production ended in 1984 following the launch of the new Renault 5.

* The Renault 5 was available only in three-door form until 1980, when a five-door version that used the 7's rear door design was launched.

## G34

*What was the name of the coupé produced by Saab in the 1960s and 1970s?*

**D.     Sonett**

Although the Saab Sonnet first appeared in the 1950s, only six of the 748cc, two stroke-engined roadsters were built between 1955 and 1957, all of them being in right-hand drive form.

A new take on the Sonett, the Sonett II, appeared in 1966. Like the earlier Sonetts, it featured a glassfibre reinforced plastic body (in coupé form this time) attached to a separate chassis.

Early Sonett IIs came with an 841cc version of the three-cylinder, two-stroke engine used in the Sonett 1 but later examples, known as the Sonett V4, were fitted with a 1498cc Ford V4 engine.

The Sonett I and II were primarily intended for competition use, but the third and final version of the Sonett, the Ford V4-powered Sonett III, was aimed at a wider pool of buyers. It used the same chassis as the Sonett II/V4 but had much revised bodywork. The changes included a new front end with pop-up headlamps, a hinged rear window and, from 1972, the fitment of impact-absorbing bumpers. In addition, a larger, 1699cc version of the Ford V4 engine was fitted from 1971 onwards.

Like the Sonett II and V4 models, the Sonett III was aimed at the US market. Indeed, almost the entire production run was exported to the USA. Consequently, it was offered only in left-hand drive form.

Production ended in 1974 with a total of 8368 Sonett IIIs having been built, to add to the 258 Sonett IIs and 1610 V4s produced between 1966 and 1969.

### G35

*Which of the following cars did **not** use the same exterior door handles as the Morris Marina?*

**A.    Morris Ital**

The Morris Marina could never be accused of being a style icon but one element of its design did catch on: its exterior door handles.

It wasn't, truth be told, that the Marina's door handles were of a radical new design – the AMC AMX sported a similar type of handle in 1968, as did the Lamborghini Urraco prototype in 1970. Moreover, the early styling proposals for the Marina featured a rather different door handle than that which was fitted to production models.

Be that as it may, there's no doubt that the mass-produced Marina popularised the design. Indeed, within a few years the same door handles could be found on the Austin Allegro, Triumph TR7, Reliant Scimitar SE6, Range Rover, Land Rover Discovery and even the Lotus Esprit. And that's not all: various Alfa Romeos sported similar-looking door handles, as did the Fiat 132, Peugeot 305 and the Talbot-Matra Murena.

Ironically, the car that the Marina evolved into, the Morris Ital, did not carry over its predecessor's door handles when launched in 1980.

### G36

*In 1970, the members of England's squad for the 1970 football World Cup were each given the loan of which car?*

**A.      Ford Cortina 1600E**

How things have changed.

In 2020, the top 200+ players in the English Premier League are rewarded with salaries of £2,000,000 or more, and that's before endorsements etc. are taken into account. In 1970, however, the average weekly wage for players in the English First Division (the equivalent of today's EPL) was a princely £70 per week. And although the top players were better rewarded than that (George Best was reportedly paid £1000 per week in 1968), their lifestyles were far removed from the soccer stars of today.

Viewed in that context, the members of England's 1970 World Cup squad were unlikely to sneeze at a year's loan of a brand new Cortina 1600E with an option to buy it at a reduced price when the loan ended. Indeed, at least one of the players, Manchester City's Francis Lee, bought 'his' Cortina at the end of the loan period. He kept it for a time then traded it in…for about twice the price he paid for it.

The story of the World Cup Cortinas and their fates is the subject of an excellent book by renowned motoring journalist James Ruppert. Further details of this and his other, equally good, publications can be found on his website: www.bangernomics.com.

**G37**

*The Peugeot 309 was originally intended to be sold as the Talbot...?*

**B.     Arizona**

After purchasing Chrysler Europe in 1978, PSA hastily rationalised the former Simca and Chrysler ranges. Production of the Simca 1000 and Hillman Hunter ranges was ended, the remaining models were rebadged as 'Talbots' and some new models – the Solara, Tagora and Samba – were introduced.

Further rationalisation then followed, with the closure of the Linwood factory and the consequent ending of Avenger and Sunbeam production in 1981.

However, none of the new models made a significant impact on the market: the Tagora flopped in both the UK and mainland Europe, the Samba was based on an old design (the Peugeot 104), and the Solara was based on the ageing Simca 1307/Alpine platform.

The effects of the 1979 energy crisis and consequent recession as well as the inherited liability for Chrysler Europe's debts added to an already fairly unpromising situation and caused PSA to reconsider its three marque strategy.

One outcome of these deliberations was the cancellation of plans to replace the Talbot Horizon with a new model, the Talbot Arizona. Instead, the car that was to have been launched as the Arizona switched marque and was instead released as the Peugeot 309.

With no new models in the pipeline, the existing Talbot cars struggled on for a time until, in 1987, production of the last of them, the Horizon, came to an end. The Talbot name continued to appear for a time on badge-engineered Talbot Express vans before finally disappearing in the 1990s.

## G38

*What was the first European production car to have a turbocharged engine?*

### C. BMW 2002 Turbo

There was nothing new about turbocharging by the time that 1973 rolled around. It had been used for years in both aircraft and marine engines but the motor industry had largely ignored it.

The sea change came in 1973 when BMW introduced the 2002 Turbo. Sitting at the top of the company's 2002 model range, the Turbo was powered by a 1990cc SOHC four-cylinder engine mated to Kugelfischer mechanical fuel injection and a KKK turbocharger. In turbocharged form, the engine pumped out 170bhp, some 40bhp more than the same engine in its normally aspirated, fuel-injected form, as fitted to the 2002 Tii.

The effect on performance was startling: the 2002 Turbo could attain a top speed of 130mph and reach 60mph from a standstill in 7.3 seconds. By way of contrast, the 2002 Tii took a second longer to reach 60mph and ran out of steam at 116mph. More important in real world terms was the fact that the Turbo's in-gear acceleration times comfortably bettered those of the Tii.

The Turbo's appearance distinguished it from lesser 2002s as well, thanks to its wider wheels, large front airdam, riveted fibreglass wheel arch extensions and a boot-mounted spoiler. And then there were the decals...

For the most part, the 2002's decals were innocuous enough. Save, that is, for the '2002 Turbo' decal that was *reverse printed* on the front air dam of the pre-production show car. This meant that it could only be read by using a mirror such as, oh, the rear-view mirror of the car in front. Some elements within the German press were unhappy about this, thinking it to be irresponsible. BMW took the hint and deleted the offending decal from production cars. They didn't completely cave in to the criticism, though, as the decal remained available as a dealer-fitted option.

But if the front decal was wild, the handling wasn't. BMW had endowed the Turbo with a limited-slip differential and uprated springs and dampers. It's on-off boost characteristics could catch out the unwary, but those familiar with the car's ways found it to be a better balanced and more predictable car to drive than the Tii model.

For such a seminal car, the 2002 Turbo had a very brief production life, thanks to the effect of the global energy crisis that followed the 1973 Yom Kippur war and severely curbed the demand for powerful, thirsty cars.

Only 1672 examples had been built when production ceased in 1974.

## G39

*Which 1960s microcar was manufactured on the Isle of Man?*

**A.     Peel P50**

When you're designing a car that measures under four and half feet in length, something has to give. And that's probably why the Peel P50 came with one seat, one headlight, one windscreen wiper, no boot and and no reverse gear. Oh, and it had three wheels too.

Built between 1962 and 1965 at Peel on the Isle of Man, the P50 was (and is) road legal. That said, with a 49cc DKW engine that develops 4.2 bhp, it's best suited to urban environments in which its size and agility make up for its sub-40 mph top speed.

Given its name, it's appropriate that around 50 examples were built before production ended, over half of which still exist. Prices of the surviving examples are, however, a little steeper than the £199 it cost to buy one back in 1963. Indeed, one American-based example fetched a remarkable $176,000 at auction in 2016.

## G40

*In what car did Lord Lucan flee from the scene of his alleged crimes in 1974?*

## D. Ford Corsair

Once the most famous wanted man in the UK, the fate of Richard John Bingham, the 7th Earl of Lucan, continues to exercise the minds of would-be sleuths almost half a century after his disappearance.

Born in December 1934, the Eton-educated Lucan served in the Coldstream Guards before embarking on a short-lived career with a Merchant Bank.

Tall and moustachioed, Lucan cut quite a dash in his younger days, having a love of speed and a taste for gambling. He was a regular at the Clermont Club in London, where he met and befriended Ian Fleming, the creator of James Bond, in the early 1960s. Fleming saw something of his fictional spy in Lucan, and it has been reported that Lucan was among those considered to play James Bond on the silver screen.

Lucan's personal life was, however, nothing like that of Fleming's suave spy. By the early 1970s he was deeply in debt and his marriage was in tatters.

I don't propose to go into detail about the events of 7th November, 1974 at an address in Lower Belgrave Street, London. Suffice it to say that a young woman named Sandra Rivett, the nanny to the children of Lord and Lady Lucan, was murdered at that address. Lady Lucan was herself assaulted but managed to flee from the house and raise the alarm. She told the police that her husband was the assailant, but when officers arrived at the house he was nowhere to be seen.

Later that same night, Lord Lucan arrived at the home of friends in Uckfield, East Sussex, having driven there in a borrowed Ford Corsair rather in his own Mercedes-Benz, which had a flat battery. After speaking to one of his friends, Lucan drove off into the night and has not been seen since. The Corsair was, however, found at Newhaven, sixteen miles from his friends' home in Uckfield, three days after the last verified sighting of Lucan.

Lucan was formally declared dead in 2016, albeit no trace of him has ever been found. Various theories have been postulated as to what became of him, but his fate remains unknown. If still alive, he will celebrate his 86$^{th}$ birthday in December 2020.

# *It Pays To Advertise I*

## A1

*What car was advertised on UK television with the slogan "Not the car for Mr. Average"?*

**A.    Princess 2**

At launch in 1975, BL's new, wedge-shaped family car was offered as a Morris, an Austin and a Wolseley (the last car to bear that name), a messy marketing tactic that was very short-lived: within six months, it was sold only as a Princess.

Originally offered with a choice of the 1.8 litre B-series engine and the 2.2 litre, six-cylinder E-series unit, the Princess drew criticism for its styling and soon developed a reputation for unreliability. Most damning of all, however, was BL's decision to give it a conventional boot rather than the hatchback configuration sported by many of its chief rivals. Indeed, it was left to two small companies, Crayford of Kent and Torcars of Devon, to create hatchback* versions of the Princess.

A revamped version of the Princess, the Princess 2, was launched in 1978. It now offered 1.7 litre and 2.0 litre O-series engines in place of the venerable B-series, but BL somehow passed up the chance to turn it into a hatchback.

They did, however, mark the launch of the Princess 2 by running a TV commercial which extolled its virtues, including its large boot, and depicted other cars as grey blocks on wheels. "Not the car for Mr. Average", proclaimed the commercial. If it had been talking about sales figures then it would have been right: the Princess barely outsold the aged Maxi – indeed, it was outsold by the Maxi in 1976. Meanwhile, Mr. Average bought a Ford Cortina or Vauxhall Cavalier instead.

The Princess soldiered on until 1982, when it was replaced by a heavily revised version: the Austin Ambassador. In this new guise it finally acquired a hatchback. It was, however, a case of too little, too late, and the Ambassador was dropped in 1984 to make way for the new Austin

Montego.

* Ogle Design produced a Princess-based prototype for Triplex in 1977. This resulting Ogle Triplex 10-20 was a striking design, with opening hatch, which showed just how appealing the Princess could have been. But don't take my word for it: you can check it out at the British Motor Museum in Warwickshire.

## A2

*Which car was promoted in the UK with the slogan "Built like Rocky"?*

**B.**     **Citroën AX GT**

If you're thinking that Citroën was suggesting that their pint-sized AX resembled a certain Mr. Balboa then think again. Oh, don't get me wrong, they were comparing the AX to a heavyweight boxer, but a real-life one: Rocky Marciano.

Marciano was small for a heavyweight at 5 feet 10½ but was strong, durable and, as it proved, unbeatable. He retired with a record of 49 wins, no draws and no defeats, having won 43 of his fights inside the distance.

The AX GT commercial compared the AX's impressive power-to-weight ratio with Marciano's ability to outmuscle bigger and heavier opponents. A curious comparison, for sure, but a memorable one, and that's surely the point of any advertisement.

The AX GT enjoyed some success during its production run, but the time came when Citroën realised that more was, well, more when it came to hot (or warm) hatchbacks, and released a GTI version with an extra 15 bhp.

## A3

*Which car was advertised as "The car you always promised yourself"?*

**C.**     **Ford Capri**

The 1960s saw a proliferation of big-engined, brawny coupés in the USA. Known as 'pony cars', the likes of the Ford Mustang, Chevrolet Camaro and Dodge Charger were, however, better suited to the wide-open spaces of the USA than to the UK, not to mention the fact that the low fuel prices of the USA made feeding their thirsty V8 engines a much more viable proposition Stateside.

The question of how to give European buyers a taste of pony car style without the associated costs was answered with the launch of the Ford Capri in 1969. Featuring fastback coupé looks allied to tried and trusted mechanical components, the Capri's marketing campaign played heavily on its combination on style and affordability. It was, said Ford's ads, "The car you always promised yourself."

Whether or not the Capri quite lived up to that tag is a matter for debate, but there can no doubt about its sales appeal. It was the eighth best-selling car in the UK in the 1970s and continued in production until 1986, having been updated and revised to a greater or lesser degree at regular intervals.

Ford chose not to replace the Capri when it ended production, leaving its place in the model range to be filled by the sportier versions of the Fiesta, Escort and Sierra.

In the 1990s, Ford finally returned to the sector once occupied by the Capri. Unfortunately, neither of its two offerings, the Probe and Cougar coupés, attracted buyers in anything like the numbers that the Capri had achieved.

## A4

*The Ford Puma was advertised in the UK using footage and music lifted from which movie?*

**B.    Bullitt**

Ford pulled out all the stops in 1997 when it came to creating a TV ad that showcased its new Fiesta-based coupé, the Puma.

Using a mixture of fresh footage, digital inserts and original footage from the 1968 film *Bullitt*, a silver Puma is hustled around the streets of San Francisco to the jazzy strains of Lalo Schifrin's main theme from the film.

If that was all the commercial had to offer then it'd still have been good, but what took to another level was the digitally-revived presence of Steve McQueen, the King of Cool himself. Indeed, McQueen's image is woven so skilfully into the commercial that it's very, very hard to see the joins.

McQueen would later 'appear' in another Ford commercial, a *Field of Dreams* themed ad. for the Mustang that aired in the USA. But the Puma ad. is the one to see. In fact, I think I'll go and have a decko at it now.

## A5

*Which car company used the guitar riff from the song "Layla" in its UK television advertisements?*

**D.     Vauxhall**

There's nothing new about car companies using snippets from hit songs to market their cars. After all, it's a hugely effective way of placing a link to the product in the minds of potential customers – hear the song on the radio, automatically think of the product it advertises.

For Renault in the 1990s, the song was 'Johnny and Mary' by Robert Palmer; for Mercedes-Benz it was a reworking of Janis Joplin's 'Mercedes Benz'; for Ford, it was Brian May's 'Driven by you'; and for Vauxhall it was Eric Clapton's iconic guitar lick from 'Layla'.

You can check them all out on you tube, but be warned: once played these songs tend to stay in your head for a while. And that's exactly why the marketing people chose them.

## A6

*Whose cars were promoted by the Scotland football team in 1978?*

**D.     Chrysler**

Using the Scotland football team to promote their cars must have seemed like a good idea to Chrysler at the time. After all, Scotland was the only one of the home nations to have qualified for the 1978 World Cup and, given their creditable performance in the 1974 tournament and a squad that included a number of gifted players, it seemed that they had a decent chance of doing well in Argentina.

Accordingly, a TV commercial featuring a selection of Chrysler cars and Scotland players in a stadium (possibly White City in London) was aired, and a printed advertisement, also featuring several players, proclaimed that the (Scottish-built) Chrysler Avenger would win the World Cup for value, if there were one.

Scotland's World Cup campaign was, however, a disaster that was only partly redeemed by beating The Netherlands, who made it to the final of the tournament, in the last game of the group stages. Alas, things went no better for Chrysler, who sold off their European arm to PSA Peugeot Citroën for a nominal $1 before the year was out.

### A7

*Which car featured in a UK advertisement with the slogan "You can always say it's your wife's"?*

**B.     Citroën Dyane**

Picture, if you will, a Citroën Dyane with its sunroof open. Inside it stands a bowler-hatted city gent, leaning casually against the B-pillar. The accompanying text admits you wouldn't buy a Dyane in order to impress the neighbours before going on to talk about the features that make it such a sensible purchase. Good stuff, you think, but then you recall the headline about being able to say it belongs to your wife, and your view changes to "Oops, that won't go down well."

Rather, it wouldn't go down well nowadays. Indeed, I'm not sure that any advertising agency would even contemplate running such an ad. Things were, however, different back in the 1970s.

So much for the ad, then; what about the car?

Launched in 1967, the Dyane was essentially a hatchback version of the 2CV with different front-end styling. Its practicality was aided by its full-length fabric sunroof, thus enabling it to carry a wide variety of cargos.

The Dyane sold well but only managed to outsell its booted sibling for a couple of years, after which its sales invariably lagged behind those of the 2CV. Production ended in 1984, six years before the last 2CV was built.

For all its practical appeal, the Dyane seems, alas, to have become something of a forgotten car in the UK, with only 259 being licensed in the UK as at the second quarter of 2020.

**A8**

*"The People's Ferrari" was a slogan used to advertise which British sports car in the USA?*

**C.     MG Midget**

Time was when British sports cars had a healthy following in the USA.

America's love affair with British sports cars began in World War 2, when many a young American airman or GI based in the UK found himself entranced by the small, open-top sports cars made by the likes of MG. And the romance continued after a hot war was replaced by a cold one, with US forces continuing to be stationed in the UK.

Moreover, US rates of pay and a favourable exchange rate meant that US personnel could not only afford to buy a British sports car but ship it Stateside when their tour of duty in the UK was over.

The floodgates really opened, however, when the British motor industry started to ramp up exports and take advantage of the post-war demand for new cars in the likes of Australia and the USA. Indeed, for several years Britain was the world's leading exporter of cars.

This outward expansion meant that Americans with a taste for British sports cars could buy them locally rather than having to personally import them. And so the love affair continued, with MGs and Triumphs heading Stateside in their thousands.

It all changed, of course, but for a time the USA was the biggest market for British sports cars. Even the humble MG Midget sold well there, and with good reason: the Midget was cheap to buy and run and offered sporty, open-top motoring in a country in which sunshine isn't the stranger that it can be in the UK.

Calling it a 'People's Ferrari' might just have been taking it a bit far, though!

## A9

*Which singing star appeared (and sang) in a UK TV commercial for the Chrysler Sunbeam?*

**D.     Petula Clark**

The Chrysler Sunbeam was something of an automotive urchin: a stop-gap car with an outmoded drivetrain that was rushed into production.

Lumbered with a rear-wheel drive configuration that adversely impacted on its space efficiency, the Sunbeam was nonetheless a pleasant enough little car. But in a time of economic strife and facing stiff competition, it needed all the help it could get.

At its launch in 1977, Chrysler's marketing team plumped for the sunny day, open road theme in its TV advertising while Petula Clark warbled in the background about 'putting a Chrysler Sunbeam in your life'. Alas, the song chosen for Ms. Clark wasn't a patch on her big 1960s hits. A version that replaced 'Chrysler' with 'little' was released as a single but failed to chart.

Sadly for the Sunbeam, it too failed to find the audience that it – and Chrysler Europe - so desperately needed, although a production run of around 200,000 cars in four years was nothing to be ashamed of. And, in

Lotus-engined guise, it won the World Rally Championship for the Talbot team in 1981.

## A10

*Which Hollywood star appeared in the UK TV commercial for the Ford Cougar in the late 1990s?*

**A.** **Dennis Hopper**

Largely forgotten now, the Mondeo-based Cougar was intended to offer coupé style to buyers who needed more space than the Puma could provide.

Launched in 1998 with a choice of either 2.0 litre four-cylinder or 2.5 litre V6 engines, the Cougar went and handled well enough but was perhaps hampered a little by Ford's somewhat polarising (at the time) *New Edge* styling.

Following as it did on the heels of the Puma, it's perhaps no surprise that, for the Cougar, Ford sought to repeat the success of the Puma's advertising campaign by lifting images and music from another film from the late 1960s, *Easy Rider*.

The resulting advertisement featured Dennis Hopper driving a Cougar in company with a chopper-style motorbike ridden by Billy, the character he played in *Easy Rider*. Again, the soundtrack featured music taken from the source film, this time Steppenwolf's classic 'Born to be Wild'.

It was a decent enough commercial but failed to reach the heights achieved by the Puma commercial, much in the same way as the Cougar was outshone by its smaller sibling.

# General Knowledge V

## G41

*What nickname was given to the Renault 14 in France?*

**B.    La poire**

Introduced in 1976, the Renault 14 was a mid-sized hatchback that sat directly above the Renault 5 in the Renault range.

Offered only as a five-door hatchback, the 14 came with a choice of two engines, 1.2 litre and 1.4 litre versions of the joint Peugeot-Renault X-Type engine, also known as the *Douvrin* or *suitcase* engine. As it turned out, however, the 14 was the only Renault to use X-Type engines.

One of Renault's advertisements for the 14 pictured it within the outline of a pear. Consequently, it became known in France as '*la poire*', although its susceptibility to premature rust later resulted in it being called 'the rotten pear' by the motoring press.

Sales failed to live up to Renault's hopes, but even so nearly 1,000,000 examples had rolled off the production line by the time that production ceased in 1983.

Never a big seller in this side of the channel\*, just 14 examples are known to remain in the UK, with only 7 of them being licensed as at the second quarter of 2020.

\*As an aside, a 14 appeared in several episodes of the 1970s TV series, *Shoestring*.

## G42

*What was the name of the rotary-engined Citroën that was based on the Ami 8?*

**A.    M35**

In 1964 Citroën entered into a joint venture with German carmaker NSU to develop rotary engine technology. Three years later, the two companies went a step further and a new engine manufacturer, Comotor, was born. And two years after that, the first rotary engined Citroën hit the streets.

This car, the M35, was based on the company's Ami 8, but had hydropneumatic suspension and two doors rather than four. Moreover, under the bonnet lay a small, single rotor engine built by Comotor. The engine was the M35's raison d'etre, its purpose being to act as a real-world test bed for this new technology.

Citroën's plan for the M35 was original: 500 M35s would be sold to specially selected customers who would each agree to cover a minimum of 18,500 miles a year in their M35 and have their cars serviced only by Citroën dealers. In this way, the performance and reliability of the M35 fleet could be monitored and the results fed back to the Citroën and Comotor technical departments.

As it turned out, only 267* M35s were built, each of which had its individual number printed on the front wings. The fleet, although smaller in number than planned, generated a substantial amount of useful data, and in that respect the project was a success.

At the end of the test programme, Citroën bought back and destroyed many of the M35 prototypes. Even so, it's believed that as many as 90 may still exist, albeit in various states of roadworthiness.

The M35 wasn't the only Citroën to be powered by a rotary engine; it was followed by the GS Birotor of 1973, which briefly went into series production. But that's another story...

*Don't be fooled by Citroën's numbering system, which skipped a couple of hundred numbers, thus making it appear that 500 M35s had been built.

## G43

*What was the first production car to have a mid-mounted engine?*

**B.** **Bonnet Djet**

The Bonnet Djet was the brainchild of René Bonnet, a French engineer who had, in tandem with his compatriot Charles Deutsch, produced a succession of attractive sports cars under the Deutsch-Bonnet banner.

In 1961, however, Deutsch and Bonnet went their separate ways. Deutsch went into business as C-D while Bonnet founded Automobiles René Bonnet.

A year later, Bonnet launched the Djet, a pretty, two-seat coupé with a mid-mounted 1108cc Renault engine, all-round independent suspension, disc brakes on all four wheels and a glassfibre body mounted on a steel chassis.

There were two models: the 65bhp Djet 1 and the 80bhp Djet 2. Both could exceed 100mph. Deliveries commenced in July, 1963, shortly after a modified Djet, known as the Aerodjet, had won the coveted Index of Thermal Efficiency at the Le Mans 24 Hours. Sales, however, were lower than Bonnet had projected, to the extent that his company found itself in serious financial difficulties.

Unable to stay afloat, the company was sold in 1964 to a creditor, Engins Matra, an aerospace and defence company. Matra quickly created a new subsidiary, Matra Sports, and production of the Djet, in a slightly modified form and now badged as a Matra-Bonnet, resumed.

The Bonnet name and the 'D' from 'Djet' were both dropped for the final version, the 1255cc Matra Jet 6. Production ended in 1967, with the Jet being replaced by a sports car of Matra's own design, the M530.

*The correct pronunciation of 'Djet' is 'Jet'. Bonnet added the 'D', as he believed that it ensured that native French speakers pronounced 'jet' properly.

**G44**

*The Citroën DS is credited with saving the life of which political leader?*

**D.**     **Charles De Gaulle**

It's fair to say that the Citroën DS didn't just push the envelope, it charged at with a battering ram. Styled by an automotive designer with a passion for sculpture, its low-drag, avant-garde shape was the perfect fusion of modern art and physics.

And if it looked striking then the technology it packed was even more impressive. It was the first mass-produced car to feature front disc brakes, and its self-levelling suspension handled the rutted roads of contemporary Europe (and 21$^{st}$ century Britain) with aplomb. It had power-assisted steering and brakes, clutchless manual transmission, unstressed, easily removable outer body panels, a lightweight fibreglass roof to help keep the centre of gravity low and an interior that made extensive and innovative use of synthetic materials.

That's an impressive specification even today, but in 1955 it didn't just change the game, it rewrote the rulebook. More than six decades on, its impact has yet to be matched, let alone bettered.

But the significance of this car wasn't limited to the motor industry. In a France ravaged by two world wars, it became a national symbol of technological and economic recovery. Moreover, it saved the life of President De Gaulle.

Feeling were running high in France in the early 1960s over the future of the French colony of Algeria. Since 1954, Algeria had been the locus of a war of a vicious, brutal and bloody war of independence. This eventually resulted in President De Gaulle opening discussions with the Algerian National Liberation Front, thereby paving the way for Algeria to regain its independence from France as well as making De Gaulle a target for the OAS, a paramilitary group opposed to the ending of French rule in Algeria.

The situation came to a head on 22$^{nd}$ August, 1962, when a dozen members of the OAS ambushed De Gaulle's small motorcade (two Citroën DSs and two motocycles) as it headed at speed along the Avenue de la Libération* in the Paris suburb of Petit-Clamart.

De Gaulle and his entourage were greeted by a veritable hail of bullets (187 shell casings were found at the scene) that killed both of the motorcycle-mounted police officers. De Gaulle's Citroën was itself struck by several rounds of ammunition, one of which narrowly missed the President's head.

Two of the DS's tyres were punctured by bullets, but although it was moving at over 60mph, De Gaulle's chauffeur was able to keep it under control and accelerate away from the ambush. That he was able to do so was due in no small part to the DS's hydropneumatic suspension system that kept the car straight and level. In a car with a conventional suspension system, the outcome for De Gaulle, France and possibly even Algeria might have been very different.

The attack on De Gaulle was recreated for the opening sequence of the 1973 film, *'The Day of the Jackal'*.

*It's now called *Avenue du Général De Gaulle*.

## G45

*Which car was mentioned in a 1977 memo to President Jimmy Carter by his Assistant for National Security Affairs?*

**B.   Matra Rancho**

In June 1977, Leonid Brezhnev, the Chairman of the Communist Party of the Soviet Union, made a state visit to France. An avid car collector, Brezhnev often returned from State visits with a new car or two that his hosts had gifted to him. Indeed, his previous visit to France had seen him return home with a new Citroën SM.

This time round, his hosts gave him two cars: a Matra-Simca Bagheera coupé and a Matra Rancho. Unfortunately, the colour of the Rancho presented to Brezhnev did not find favour with him; it was green, a colour he thought to be unlucky. He wasn't keen on the colour of the seats either, and it was quietly suggested to the French that perhaps a blue Rancho with brown seats could be offered instead.

This request was not quite as simple as it seemed, as the Rancho wasn't then available in blue. But when you're dealing with the leader of a superpower, solutions will be found. In this instance, the problem was solved by hastily sending the Rancho back to Matra's factory, repainting it blue and replacing the tan seats with brown ones.

The incident was widely reported in US newspapers and was included in a memo to President Carter by his Assistant for National Security Affairs. But don't take my word for it; the original memo can be viewed online: https://history.state.gov/historicaldocuments/frus1977-80v06/d32

### G46

*What British car was fitted with a Quartic steering wheel?*

**D.     Austin Allegro**

As the replacement for the hugely popular (it was the best-selling car in the UK for several years) BMC 1100/1300, the Austin Allegro had pretty big shoes to fill.

Unfortunately, it had been rushed into production, and it showed. The styling was on the dumpy side of plain; it had a boot rather than the more practical hatchback configuration; it had no more rear-seat legroom than its predecessor; it was uninspiring to drive; its build quality was mediocre; and it had what amounted to a square steering wheel.

The idea behind the Quartic steering wheel (essentially a square with curved corners) was that it enabled drivers to see the instruments. It was a laudable idea, but it looked odd and customers disliked it. Curiously, the Vanden Plas 1500 (a plusher version of the Allegro) came with a round steering wheel rather than a Quartic one.

BL eventually got the message about the Quartic wheel and it was dropped after a couple of years. They also set about the task about turning the Allegro into the car it should have been from the start.

It received its first major revisions with the launch of the series 2 in 1975 and was further improved when a third series was introduced in 1979.

These changes did much to improve the Allegro, but it never sold in anything like the same numbers as its predecessor.

It could so easily have been a very different story.

### G47

*Which French car company had a factory at Slough?*

**A.    Citroën**

Although Citroën's factory in Slough opened in 1926, its origins lay to some degree in the imposition of customs duties (known as *McKenna Duties* after the Chancellor of the Exchequer who imposed them) on luxury goods, including cars.

The McKenna Duties were imposed in 1915 in order to help fund the war effort but remained in effect after hostilities ceased. They were briefly repealed in 1924, reimposed in 1925 and finally removed in 1955.

By the mid-1920s, Citroën had not only sold around 25,000 vehicles in the UK but had also established a UK base at Hammersmith to deal with the importation and distribution of vehicles. That being so, it seemed logical to set up a manufacturing operation in the UK and circumvent the McKenna Duties to which imported cars were liable.

Citroën chose Slough as the location for its UK factory. Based in the Slough Trading Estate, it opened in February, 1926 and went on to produce some of Citroën's most famous cars, including the Traction Avant, 2CV, DS and Ami 6.

It also produced a model made specially for the UK market: the Bijou, a 2 door, fibreglass-bodied coupé based on the 2CV chassis. Styled by Peter Kirwan-Taylor, who also styled the original (1957) Lotus Elite, the Bijou was a resounding flop, with just 207 being built between 1959 and 1964.

The Citroën factory at Slough outlived the Bijou by a year. Some of the former factory buildings were later taken over by Mars, the confectionery manufacturer, but no trace of the old Citroën factory now remains.

## G48

*The Alfa Romeo Arna was produced as a joint venture with which other car manufacturer?*

**D.   Nissan**

In retrospect, the Arna never stood a chance. It was, after all, a car that combined the style of 1980s Nissans with 1980s Italian build quality.

It was the fruit of a 1980 agreement between Alfa Romeo and Nissan that led to the creation of A.R.N.A. (*Alfa Romeo Nissan Autoveicoli*), a 50/50 joint venture between the companies. For Alfa Romeo, A.R.N.A. offered the chance to get a new small hatchback to the market quickly and cheaply, and for Nissan it offered a way round the import quotas imposed by European countries.

A factory was constructed near Naples and production of the new car, the Alfa Romeo Arna*, commenced in 1983. The Arna itself was based on the body of the Nissan Cherry (the body panels were made in Japan and sent to Italy for assembly) and, with the notable exception of its rear suspension and rear brakes, used Alfa Romeo mechanical components.

The Arna was an intriguing idea that served, alas, to showcase the worst elements of its makers. Its build quality was poor, it was susceptible to rust, its electrics hosted a number of gremlins, its frumpy styling was not what people expected from a car wearing an Alfa Romeo badge, and its handling failed to live up to the standards set by the Alfasud. Consequently, sales were very poor indeed.

Its fate, and that of the Alfa-Nissan collaboration, was sealed when state-owned Alfa Romeo's losses became too much for the Italian government to bear. Fiat therefore stepped in and added Alfa Romeo to its portfolio. Within a short time, Alfa's alliance was Nissan was ended and Arna production ceased, with just over 53,000 having been built between 1983 and 1987.

*It was also sold as the Nissan Cherry Europe in some markets.

## G49

*Under what name was the Fiat Strada marketed in its native Italy?*

**C.     Ritmo**

The Italian language has the happy knack of making even the most mundane thing sound exotic. Indeed, that was certainly the case with the Fiat Strada. Ah, perhaps I'd better clarify that: the car wasn't mundane but the name was - *Strada* simply means *street* or *road* in Italian.

Of course, the Strada was only sold under that name in the UK, Canada and the USA. It was known as the Ritmo everywhere else.

As to the reason behind its change of name, it's been suggested that Ritmo was thought to be just too Italianate for English-speaking markets, but the fact that Fiat used it in Ireland sits squarely at odds with that theory.

But irrespective of what name it was marketed under, the Strada was an appealing car, although the restyled second series lost something of the original model's flair by dispensing with its distinctive grille and headlamp design.

The Strada (or, if your prefer, Ritmo) remained in production for 11 years (1978 to 1989) and gave rise to two very decent hot hatchbacks - the 105TC and 130TC models - as well as a memorable UK TV commercial that highlighted the use of robots in its construction and was subsequently lampooned in a classic *Not the Nine O' Clock News* sketch.

## G50

*Which of the following cars was **not** fitted with the PRV V6 engine?*

**B.     Volvo 850**

As its initials suggest, the PRV V6 engine was developed jointly by Peugeot, Renault and Volvo. Built at Douvrin in France, the engine first appeared in the Volvo 264 in 1974. Other installations quickly followed, and by the end of 1975 the PRV V6 was also available in the Peugeot 504 and 604, the Renault 30TX and the Alpine-Renault A310.

Having started out life with a displacement of 2664cc, the unit was subsequently produced in a range of capacities from 2458cc up to 2975cc. A turbocharged version first appeared in 1984, making its debut in the Renault 25 V6 Turbo.

Aside from Peugeots, Renaults and Volvos, the PRV V6 could also be found in the De Lorean DMC-12, the Lancia Thema, Dodge Monaco, Eagle Premier, and the MVS Venturi (later, Venturi) sports cars.

One car it did not appear in, however, was the Volvo 850, launched in 1992. Instead, the 850 utilised a new range of Volvo engines, in four and five-cylinder, normally aspirated and turbocharged guises.

The PRV unit continued in production until the late 1990s, gradually being phased out in favour of the new Peugeot-Renault ESL engine which made its debut in the Peugeot 406 Coupe of 1997.

# The People

## P1

*Which political leader is said to have crashed his Rolls-Royce Silver Shadow into a truck?*

**A.    Leonid Brezhnev**

During his 18 years as leader of the USSR, Leonid Brezhnev built up a remarkable collection of cars, many of which were given to him by other heads of state. For example, he was gifted a Lincoln Continental by President Nixon of the USA and a Citroën SM by President De Gaulle of France.

However, the car we're concerned with is a Rolls-Royce Silver Shadow which he received from Queen Elizabeth II in 1966. It's said that Brezhnev was particularly fond of his Silver Shadow and liked to take it for a spin from time to time, causing no small amount of headaches for his bodyguards.

It's claimed, however, that his love affair with the car came to a crashing (pun intended) halt in 1980. Having taken it out for a drive around Moscow one evening, Brezhnev had the misfortune to slam into a truck that pulled out in front of him without warning. The Silver Shadow's crumple zones did their duty and ensured that Brezhnev escaped serious injury.

The Silver Shadow was never repaired (Rolls-Royce specialists weren't exactly thick on the ground on the eastern side of the Iron Curtain) but survived Brezhnev's death in 1982. It currently resides in 'just crashed' form at a motor museum in Riga, complete with a mannequin of Brezhnev in the driver's seat.

The car is real but can the same be said about the story of Brezhnev's crash?

Possibly.

## P2

*Which motoring journalist ran a turbocharged Citroën 2CV in the 1980s?*

**C.     Steve Cropley**

A turbocharged 2CV? Surely not?

But if you were Steve Cropley, the Editor of *Car* magazine in the 1980s, your *Deux Chevaux* (known as 'The Struggler') most certainly had forced induction. In its 'blown' form, The Struggler's power output was a heady 46 bhp, sufficient to lop 14 seconds off the time it took to hit 60mph from rest and give it a top speed of close to 90 mph.

The story of how it came about is one that's best told by Steve Cropley himself. Suffice it to say, however, that the addition of a Garrett T2 turbocharger to the 2CV's air-cooled 602cc engine was no easy feat, and it took someone of the calibre of Turbo Technics' Richard Wilshere to make it work.

The resulting 2CV Turbo was tractable, docile and, when pressed, loud. So loud in fact that Richard Wilshere decided not to take it beyond 6500 rpm when measuring its power output on a rolling road.

Unfortunately, its engine caught fire whilst heading along the M1 after a photoshoot. The occupants and their photography gear escaped unscathed but the front section of the car was well cooked.

Undeterred, Messrs. Cropley and Wilshere decided to rebuild the car. It ran again, albeit with a different carburettor and a little less boost. That was more than three decades ago, though, and *The Struggler* has been off the road for many years.

It still exists and is currently on SORN, so maybe, just maybe, it'll run again someday.

## P3

*Who styled the Lotus Elite and Eclat models introduced in the mid-*

*1970s?*

**B.    Oliver Winterbottom**

Lotus founder Colin Chapman was not a man for standing still, a characteristic that lay very much at the heart of his decision to abandon the small sports cars with which the company had made its name and instead produce cars that would compete at the upper end of the sporting car market.

This process started in 1967, when a specification for a four-seat executive sports car was devised. The car should be able to sprint from zero to 60 mph in under ten seconds and go on to a top speed of 125 miles per hour. It would be light, too, with a kerb weight of under 1900 pounds.

A design for the new car was produced by John Frayling, best known for his work with Lola. Frayling's proposal was not implemented, however, and the project was thereafter placed in the hands of Oliver Winterbottom, previously of Jaguar.

Winterbottom wasted little time in producing a design for a shooting brake that was striking in its modernity – soft curves having given way to crisp angles. It met with a favourable reaction from the Lotus board and was subsequently approved for development into a production car.

When it emerged in that guise in 1974, it was powered not by the small Ford and Renault engines of previous Lotuses, but by Lotus's new type 907 engine. With a capacity of 1973cc and a power output of just under 160 bhp, the Elite, as the new car was named, was the most powerful Lotus road car to date.

It needed that power too, as with a kerb weight of 2430 pounds it comfortably exceeded the 1900 pounds that Lotus's original design specification had mandated. That said, it met the specification in terms of top speed and comfortably bettered it in terms of acceleration from a standing start.

A coupé version, the Eclat, joined the Lotus range in 1975. Both models survived until the 1980s, with an updated version of the Eclat, the Excel, remaining in production until 1992.

As for Oliver Winterbottom, he went on to design another seminal wedge-shaped car, the TVR Tasmin. He later returned to Lotus and styled the M90 prototype, the last design commissioned by Colin Chapman prior to his death in 1982.

## P4

*Music producer Giorgio Moroder was involved with the company that manufactured which supercar?*

**C.    Cizeta V16T**

If ever a car typified the 1980s credo that more is, well, more, it has to be the Cizeta V16T. Or, to use its original name, the Cizeta-Moroder V16T.

The V16T was the brainchild of Claudio Zampolli, a former Lamborghini test and development engineer who had moved to California and set himself up as an importer of high-performance cars.

To produce his own supercar, Zampolli was aided and abetted by an all-star selection of his former Lamborghini colleagues: Oliviero Pedrazzi, Achille Bevini, Ianose Bronzatti and Giancarlo Guerra.

To style the car, Zampolli turned to Marcello Gandini. And as it happened, Gandini had a ready-made design for a mid-engined supercar in his back pocket – his original styling proposal for what became the Lamborghini Diablo. This had, however, been deemed to be a little too sharp by the brass at Chrysler, Lamborghini's new owner. Accordingly, they had instructed Chrysler's in-house design team to soften it, a decision which reportedly annoyed the Italian design maestro.

With design and engineering taken care of, all that was required was someone who was able to invest in the project and who, ideally, had a contacts book full of the sort of people who had the wherewithal and inclination to buy the sharpest and hottest supercar on the market. That man was Giorgio Moroder, an Italian songwriter and music producer who had achieved fame and fortune as a leading pioneer of disco music.

The car that emerged - the Cizeta-Moroder V16T - was first shown publicly in Los Angeles in 1988. It looked every bit the definitive 1980s supercar, with its striking, cab-forward bodywork boasting two pairs of vertically stacked headlamps and prominent side strakes.

And it was just as impressive under the skin, with a 6.0 litre sixteen-cylinder engine with eight camshafts (essentially two flat-plane V8 engines sharing a common block) mounted transversely just ahead of the rear axle. Power output was quoted as 540 bhp and top speed was said to be a smidgeon over 200 mph. Heady stuff, even at an expected price of around $280,000.

But when the production car emerged in 1991 it was now known simply as the Cizeta V16T, Moroder having left the project the preceding year. The V16T was well-engineered and nicely finished, but at around $300,000 it was twice as expensive as its main competitor, the Lamborghini Diablo. Worse still, it was launched during a worldwide financial crisis.

Sales fell disastrously short of expectations and production ended in 1995. There have since been a couple of attempts at reviving the V16T, though neither has succeeded. That said, Claudio Zampolli might be willing to build you a new V16T (in coupé or Spyder form) if you can find the requisite funds.

Time to look down the back of the sofa?

## P5

*Which Lotus employee did much of the stunt driving of the Lotus Esprit in the 1977 film, 'The Spy Who Loved Me'?*

**B.**    **Roger Becker**

Having joined Lotus as an assembly line worker in 1966, Roger Becker probably never imagined that a decade later he'd be driving the company's flagship product in a James Bond film. But that's exactly what happened.

Becker's stay on the Lotus assembly line was a short one and he soon found himself on the vehicle development team – Colin Chapman recognised talent when he saw it.

In September 1976, Becker was sent to Sardinia by Chapman to act as Lotus's man on the James Bond set, with a remit that included instructing the stunt driver on how to get the best out of the Esprit. However, the stunt driver was used to heavy, front-engined American cars and found it hard to apply his talents to the light, mid-engined Lotus, to the frustration of all concerned.

That all changed one day when the Esprit's presence was summarily requested on set. With the stunt driver nowhere to be seen, Roger Becker jumped in the car and hotfooted it up the hill to where the film crew was waiting. Becker's deft handling of the Esprit did not pass unnoticed, and he was recruited to drive it in the film from that point on.

Roger Becker remained with Lotus for the rest of his career, becoming the company's Director of Vehicle Engineering.

## P5

*Which pop star crashed an Austin Maxi into a ditch on a trip to the Scottish highlands in 1969?*

**C.    John Lennon**

It can't have taken long for John Lennon to realise that a Mini wasn't the ideal vehicle in which to undertake a 700 mile drive from Surrey to the north of Scotland, particularly as said Mini was loaded with two adults, two children and their luggage.

Little wonder, then, that he stopped off at his aunt's home in Liverpool and asked his record company to provide him with something better suited to such a trip. The staff at Apple Records duly obliged, and within a few hours the Beatle and his family were able to look forward to making the rest of the journey in the spacious new Austin Maxi recently purchased by Apple as a staff car.

They made it to their destination without incident, but calamity struck on a sightseeing trip. As Lennon negotiated a single-track road, he rounded a bend to find a car heading towards him. Spooked by this, he took evasive action that resulted in the Maxi ploughing headfirst into a ditch.

None of the occupants sustained serious injury, although Lennon, Yoko Ono and Yoko Ono's daughter, Kyoko, sustained facial injuries that required treatment at Lawson Memorial Hospital in Golspie. The other occupant, Julian Lennon, escaped physical injury but was treated for shock.

Once recovered, Lennon joined the rest of the Beatles to record their Abbey Road album. Less than a year later, he quit the band. As for the Maxi, it was taken to Lennon's home in Surrey, where it stood in the garden for a time – a large, somewhat battered souvenir of a holiday that didn't quite go to plan.

## P7

*What car was closely associated with Princess Anne during the 1970s and 1980s?*

**C.     Reliant Scimitar GTE**

Princess Anne's combined 20th birthday and Christmas present from her parents had a big impact on her. It was a Reliant Scimitar GTE made to special order.

The Princess fell in love with the Scimitar to such a degree that she purchased a string of them over the years. Indeed, she still owns the GTE (her eighth) which she bought in 1988. This one was, however, built by Middlebridge rather than Reliant.

Scimitar production ended when Middlebridge folded in 1990. However, Graham Walker Ltd. holds the manufacturing rights to the Scimitar and, as such, could make one to order.

Princess Anne's fondness for the Scimitar isn't the only reason why it came to be so closely associated with her. In 1977, she made the news after being convicted of speeding in one - a rather bigger deal then than it would be now.

## P8

*Derek Robinson became infamous in the 1970s as a trade union official at which car manufacturer?*

**D.     British Leyland**

If you lived through the 1970s then you'll know that strikes were an everyday occurrence in the United Kingdom. From nurses to teachers, and miners to lorry drivers, just about everyone who could go on strike seemed to do so at one point or another.

This was no less true of the motor industry, with strikes taking place at every major car manufacturer in the UK. This led to one particular union official becoming a public figure: Derek Robinson, perhaps better known by the name the press bestowed on him, *Red Robbo*.

A member of the Communist Party, Robinson had worked his up the ranks of the Amalgamated Engineering Union, so that by 1975 he was the union convener at British Leyland's Longbridge plant in Birmingham. His notoriety stemmed from his role in leading 523 walkouts at Longbridge in a period of just thirty months.

Robinson's relationship with BL management came to a head in 1979 after he put his name to a pamphlet that criticised the company's management. He was asked to remove his name from the pamphlet but declined to do so, whereupon his employment with BL was terminated. Robinson's fate was sealed when a ballot on a proposed strike in sympathy with his sacking was heavily defeated.

## P9

*In 1983, which prominent UK politician survived a motorway crash that wrecked his brand new Ford Sierra?*

A.     Neil Kinnock

Only a few months before becoming the leader of the Labour Party, Neil Kinnock was very fortunate to walk away from a crash on the M4.

The politician was driving from Wales to London when he lost control of his recently acquired Ford Sierra. The car ascended a banking and performed a series of somersaults before sliding along the carriageway on its roof.

The car sustained extensive damage but Kinnock, who was wearing his seat belt, sustained only minor cuts and bruises and did not require to attend hospital. He was unable to explain how the accident happened beyond stating the car "just went out of control".

One suggestion for the cause of the accident is that Kinnock's Sierra was hit by a crosswind, which caused him to lose control of it. It's a plausible (albeit unproven) theory, given that early Sierras were not the most aerodynamically stable cars in a crosswind, an issue which Ford addressed by adding a small flap at the back of the rear window.

## P10

*What car did Yuri Gagarin, the first human in space, receive as a gift from France in 1965?*

D.     Matra-Bonnet Djet VS

In 1965, Major Yuri Gagarin, who made history when he rode the Vostok 1 rocket into space, visited the Paris Air Show. There he met up with two American astronauts, Ed White and James McDivitt.

Gagarin did not leave Paris empty handed, for the French government gifted him a brand new Bonnet-Matra Djet VS sports car. Gagarin was later photographed with the car in Moscow, although he is said to have used it sparingly. A modest man, he felt a little self-conscious about driving such an expensive car in a communist country.

Sadly, Gagarin was killed in an air crash in 1968. His Djet was thereafter placed on display at Star City, where Russian cosmonauts have undergone training since the 1960s. At some point in the 1990s, however, it was sold to a Lithuanian collector.

It is believed to still exist but is not on public display.

# General Knowledge VI

## G51

*The Ferrari 208 GTB and GTS were primarily intended for sale in which territory?*

**C.     Italy**

For many years, new car taxation in Italy was principally based on engine capacity. As cars with engines of over 2000cc were subject to purchase tax at a punitive rate (38% of their basic price as opposed to 18% for cars with engines of less than 2 litres), it made sense for manufacturers of big-engined cars to offer special models for the Italian market.

In the case of the Ferrari 208, it was equipped with a 1990cc version of the 308's flat-plane V8 engine. Unfortunately, this reduction in capacity also meant a drop in power and, consequently, performance. The 208 still looked great, of course, but with only 152 bhp on tap it was no fireball.

As the Italian tax system penalised engine capacity rather than power, Ferrari's solution was to add a turbocharger to the 1990cc engine, thereby creating their first turbocharged road car. In this form, the 208 had a healthy 217 bhp on tap, making it very nearly as rapid as its larger-engined sibling.

Other manufacturers also created special 2.0 litre versions of their larger-engined cars, notably Alfa Romeo who produced a 2.0 litre turbocharged version of their glorious V6 *Busso* engine for use in several models, including the 164 and GTV.

Oh, and if you're wondering, Italy's new car taxation laws changed some years ago, thus bringing an end to the 2.0 litre special models.

## G52

*The Panther 6 was so-called because...?*

**A.     It had six wheels**

It would be wrong to say that there was a rash of six-wheel cars in the 1970s, but there were at least three that are worthy of note: the Tyrrell P34, which won a Grand Prix in 1976; the Hustler 6, a six-wheel version of William Towns' Mini-based Hustler kit car; and the Panther 6.

Designed by Panther Westwinds' supremo, Robert Jankel, the 6 was a long (16 feet), wide (nearly 7 feet) and low convertible which, like the Tyrrell P34 that had inspired its designer, featured two pairs of wheels at the front and a further pair at the rear.

Powered by a turbocharged 8.2 litre Cadillac V8 that produced a claimed (and probably a little optimistic) 600 bhp, the 6 was said to be capable of 200mph, a claim that was never put to the test.

A running prototype of the 6 was shown at the 1977 Motorfair in London. Its size, shape and luxurious interior (its equipment included digital instruments, electrically-powered seats, a telephone concealed in an armrest, a TV on the dashboard and a hydraulically-operated engine cover) drew gasps from the crowds, but so did the projected price. At nearly £40,000, its market was severely limited.

It was slated to appear in 1978 but there was still no sign of it when Panther hit financial problems in 1979. The company was saved, but Jankel was out and the new owners had no interest in pursuing the 6 beyond completing a second car that they'd acquired with the remnants of the company.

Both Panther 6's are, however, understood to still be in existence.

### G53

*What was the name of the four-wheeled Reliant that shared the same engine as the Robin?*

**B.    Kitten**

Launched in 1975, the Reliant Kitten was available in saloon, estate and van versions. Designed by Ogle and using the same 850cc engine as the Robin, the Kitten's lightweight GRP body endowed it with excellent fuel economy and nippy acceleration. Moreover, although it was the best part of a foot longer than a Mini, its turning circle was a mere 24 feet, making it ideal for city use.

Unfortunately, the Kitten's price meant that it was more expensive than many other 'budget' cars. For example, in 1978 it cost more than a Mini 1000, base model Ford Fiesta and even the larger-engined Simca 1100 as well as being considerably pricier than a Citroën 2CV or Dyane.

It was, however, regarded as a dependable little car, and had Reliant been able to sell it for the same sort of price as a 2CV it would have surely have sold in greater numbers. As it was, just over 4500 Kittens had been built when production ceased in 1982.

## G54

*What was the first mass-produced car to have a hot-dip galvanised chassis?*

**A.     Talbot-Matra Murena**

Like many cars of the 1970s, neither the Matra-Simca Bagheera nor the Matra Rancho enjoyed a good reputation for the quality of their rustproofing.

Decisive action was therefore taken by Matra to ensure that the Bagheera's replacement, the Talbot-Matra Murena, would not suffer from the same problems. The solution they hit upon was to dip the Murena chassis into a tank of molten zinc. In that way, the entire chassis, including the welds, was coated with a protective layer of zinc.

All of the 10,680 Murenas produced between 1980 and 1983 were thus treated. The process proved to be highly effective and was thereafter applied to the Espaces and Avantimes that succeeded the Murena on the Matra production lines.

## G55

*Launched in 1980, the Fiat Panda was named after...?*

**B.     A Goddess**

There's not much I can say about this one, other than to explain that the Fiat Panda was named after the Roman Goddess Empanda.

Opinion differs as to whether she was the Goddess of food or of travellers or of hospitality. However, I prefer the account that says that she was worshipped by country folk – a sort of rustic Goddess, if you will. To me, that fits the unassuming, utilitarian nature of the Fiat Panda to a tee, as well as the fact that Fiat had considered naming it Rustica...

## G56

*Which British engineering company produced the 'Tracer', an estate version of the Triumph TR7?*

**D.     Crayford**

An estate version of the TR7? Really?

Kent-based Crayford Engineering was well-known in the 1970s and 1980s for producing modified versions of mainstream cars. For example, it produced convertible versions of the Mini and Cortina, a hatchback version of the Princess, and an estate version of the Mercedes S-class.

In 1976, a BL dealer, Page Motors, commissioned Crayford to build an estate version of the Triumph TR7. They duly did so, turning the two-seat TR7 coupé into a three-door estate with 2+2 seating and a folding rear seat. Its bullet-like profile gave rise to its name: Tracer.

It may have resembled a bullet from one angle, but the Tracer's overall styling was rather less than harmonious, and although it was shown at several motor shows and driven by the motoring press, it failed to attract interest from either BL or the general public. It still exists today, its colour having been changed from yellow to red.

BL also pursued the idea of a two-box TR7, albeit their design was a hatchback rather than an estate. This car, the Lynx, was based on a stretched TR7 chassis and, like the Tracer, had a 2+2 seating arrangement. Triumph and MG versions were proposed, with the former being powered by the 3.5 litre Rover V8 engine and the latter by the 2.0 litre O-series unit.

The Lynx came agonisingly close to making it into production. The tooling was ready to install, but the closure of BL's Speke factory in 1978 following a lengthy strike brought the project to a halt before a single production car was built.

A Rover-powered prototype of the Lynx has survived, however, and is on display at the British Motor Museum.

### G57

*Which Lancia was sold in the USA as the Scorpion?*

**D.      Beta Montecarlo**

The Lancia Beta Montecarlo (later versions dropped 'Beta' from the name) was an attractive, mid-engined sports car with a 2.0 litre, 120 bhp engine and respectable performance (118mph, 0-60mph in around 8.6 seconds) by mid-1970s standards.

Unless, of course, it was a US market model.

Lancia couldn't use the 'Montecarlo' name in the USA, as Chevrolet already had a car named Monte Carlo in production. Accordingly, the Montecarlo Spider was sold Stateside as the Lancia Scorpion. Not a bad name for a mid-engined car **if** the mid-engined car in question has a sting in the tail. Sadly for Lancia, their Scorpion did not.

In order to comply with US emissions regulations, the Scorpion was equipped with a smaller (1756cc), lower-compression engine with milder camshaft profiles and a smaller carburettor. The result was a power output of a mere 81 bhp, which utterly destroyed the Scorpion's sporting pretensions. And that wasn't all – the Scorpion sported ugly, impact-absorbing bumpers and odd, quasi pop-up headlamps (again, this was to meet US regulations) and, just to add salt to its wounds, it was over 100 pounds heavier than the Montecarlo.

Unsurprisingly, the Scorpion did not sell well Stateside, and even a role as Herbie's love interest in the 1977 Disney film, *'Herbie Goes to Monte Carlo'*, couldn't attract enough buyers to make it viable for Lancia to continue to offer it in the USA.

Scorpion exports to the USA ended in 1977, after 1805 examples had been built.

### G58

*Which company best known for sporting cars also built three-wheel invalid tricycles for the UK government?*

**C.    AC**

After World War 2, the UK government introduced a scheme under which many disabled people were entitled to a government-provided vehicle. For a few, this vehicle took the form of a suitably adapted car with two seats. Most of those eligible under the scheme were, however, only entitled to a single-seater tricycle; the rationale being that tricycles were cheaper than cars.

To this end the government entered into contracts with a number of vehicle manufacturers, including AC. In the years that followed, a standard specification for invalid tricycles was produced, which included the requirement that their bodywork be a specific shade of blue.

By 1968, AC was one of the two main suppliers of invalid trikes to the government. Indeed, from 1971 onwards all invalid trikes manufactured for the government were based on an AC design, known as the Model 70.

Powered by a rear-mounted 493cc engine and with variable belt transmission, the Model 70 could be driven as quickly in reverse as it could in forward gear. A few Model 70s were fitted with 650cc engines, which gave them a top speed of over 80 miles per hour – a scary prospect in a vehicle known for its susceptibility to crosswinds.

The provision of invalid trikes was long a matter of debate, with questions raised about not only their safety but also the fairness of providing a single-seat trike to disabled persons with families.

The axe finally fell in 1976, when the UK government decided to end the provision of invalid trikes and introduce a new state benefit, Mobility Allowance. Accordingly, Trike production was to cease by no later than 1978, with all trikes (these being the property of the government rather than their keeper) being removed from the road by the end of 1981.

This was a hammer blow that heralded the end of an era for AC Cars, which was then struggling to get its new sports car, the 3000ME, into production. Over the next few years, AC left its iconic premises in Thames Ditton High Street, ceased vehicle production and was sold.

The invalid trikes continued in service to 2003, far beyond the original date for their withdrawal. The vast majority of them were scrapped, but a few escaped the net. Indeed, some have been re-registered as tricycles so that they can once again be used on UK roads.

### G59

*Which car gave rise to a limited edition 'Jeans' model (complete with denim seat covers) in the 1970s?*

**D.     VW Beetle**

Forget haute couture, the 1970s was all about blue denim.

Denim was cool and people loved it. The streets were a sea of denim jeans, shirts, jackets, hot pants, dresses, dungarees and even suits. It was enough to make a grand couturier weep.

It was therefore a bit of a no-brainer for VW to cash-in on the public's affection for denim by releasing a special 'Jeans' edition of the hugely popular Beetle in 1973. Based on the 1200 model, the UK version of the

'Jeans' edition came in a single colour: Tunis Yellow. Apart from its colour, a 'Jeans' Beetle could be distinguished by its Lemmertz sports wheels and the black decals, which included the word 'Jeans', that ran along the side of its body.

Inside, the seats had blue denim covers with yellow stitching, and there were pockets in the front seat backrests. The door cards were also blue but were covered in vinyl rather than denim.

1600 Jeans Beetles were sold in the UK in 1973 and 1974, but none of the later editions offered elsewhere were officially imported to the UK.

## G60

*The Hillman Avenger was sold in the USA as the ...?*

**B.    Plymouth Cricket**

The Hillman Avenger was the only all-new* car to be developed by Chrysler United Kingdom following Chrysler's takeover of Rootes in 1967.

Launched in 1970, the Avenger took its styling cues from contemporary American cars, particularly its 'coke-bottle' waistline. The result was a shape that was pleasing to prospective buyers on both sides of the Atlantic. Renamed the Plymouth Cricket, it went on sale in the USA less than a year after its launch in Europe.

Built at Ryton-in-Dunsmore near Coventry, the first shipment of Crickets reached the USA at the end of 1970. There was only one engine offered – the all-iron 1498cc OHV unit fitted to some UK market Avengers – and it was initially only available as a four-door saloon; an estate version followed in 1972.

The Cricket enjoyed some sporting success in the USA, winning the 1971 Press-On-Regardless Rally, but sales were harder to come by. Its small engine was unlikely to appeal to a market used to rumbling V8s, build quality was something of a bugbear and the sheer distance between the UK and USA created logistical headaches in terms of the availability of spare parts.

With another Chrysler import, the Dodge Colt (a rebadged Mitsubishi Colt Galant) doing rather better, the plug was pulled on the Cricket in 1972, though it continued to be marketed until 1973.

The Avenger lasted rather longer in its native UK. Rebadged first as a Chrysler then as a Talbot, it was built until in 1981.

* The Chrysler Sunbeam was based on a shortened Avenger platform.

# Film & TV II

### F11

*In what year was 'Top Gear' first broadcast in the UK?*

**D.    1977**

Presented by Angela Rippon and Tom Coyne, the first episode of Top Gear was broadcast on BBC 2 on 22$^{nd}$ April, 1977.

In its original guise, the show was very much fact-based and focused on road tests, consumer advice, road safety and motoring news. It stuck to much the same magazine-based format over the next 24 years, although its style and tone became somewhat more irreverent as time passed, particularly after Jeremy Clarkson became a regular presenter in 1990.

Viewing figures began to slip towards the end of the 1990s, the decline being at least partly attributable to Clarkson's departure in early 1999, and it was cancelled in December 2001.

It returned in a new format in October 2002 and has since remained a staple of BBC 2's output.

### F12

*Which Hollywood film star raced a Mini in a round of the British Saloon Car Championship?*

**C.    Steve McQueen**

The King of Cool was pretty handy behind the wheel of a car as well as on a motorbike.

As a racer, he's best remembered for finishing second, as co-driver to Peter Revson, in the 1970 Sebring 12 Hours, the second round of that year's World Sportscar Championship. Revson, the faster of the two by some margin, did most of the driving that day but McQueen, whose foot was in plaster, didn't embarrass himself at the wheel of his Porsche 908.

That race took place at the height of McQueen's fame, but he was riding high on the success of *The Magnificent Seven* when he drove a Mini in the final round of the 1961 British Saloon Car Championship.

McQueen, who was in the UK to film *The Great Escape*, had formed a friendship with Sir John Whitmore, one of the biggest stars of UK saloon car racing. As Whitmore had already wrapped-up the BSCC title prior to its final round at Brands Hatch, he loaned his Mini to McQueen for the race.

Racing for class honours against a clutch of other Minis, McQueen was in contention for the class lead for almost the entire duration of the race, but lost out in the end to Vic Elford (who went on to enjoy great success in both rallying – he won the Monte Carlo Rally and was European Rally Champion in 1967 – and sports car racing, in which his victories included the Daytona 24 Hours, Targa Florio and Sebring 12 Hours) and Christabel Carlisle.

Elford came to know McQueen quite well and later observed that the American had the skill required to become a professional racing driver had he wished to do so.

### F13

*Who directed the classic 1984 TV advert for Shell that featured a Porsche 944, a quiet filling station and an empty road?*

**B.    Tony Scott**

You'll probably remember the ad. if you're a petrolhead of a certain age.

A Porsche 944 pulls into a small Shell filling station situated amid some striking scenery (the Ribblehead Viaduct is visible in some shots). The driver fills up, goes into the kiosk, selects a music cassette and pays for his purchases. He then enters the Porsche, pops on a pair of sunglasses, inserts the cassette into the car's radio-cassette unit, puts his seatbelt on, snicks the 944 into gear and hightails it down the open road to the accompaniment of Steppenwolf's 'Born To Be Wild'.

It's a well shot, crisply edited and stylish commercial that was directed by Tony Scott, the man who was also responsible for Saab's equally memorable *'Nothing on Earth comes close'* TV commercial.

Little wonder, then, that Scott went on to helm a string of big-budget Hollywood movies (including *Top Gun, Beverly Hills Cop II, Crimson Tide and Déjà Vu*) over the next 25 years.

## F14

*What car does the main character, Kowalski, drive in the 1971 film 'Vanishing Point'?*

**C.    Dodge Challenger R/T**

Less than three years after the Dodge Charger starred in *Bullitt's* iconic car chase, it was the turn of its slightly smaller sibling, the Challenger R/T, to feature in some fast and frantic action on the silver screen.

I don't want to spoil the film's plot, so suffice it to say that the Challenger plays an integral role in the film, it being the car that Kowalski, a car delivery driver with an intriguing past, is tasked with driving from Denver to San Francisco.

Chrysler loaned several Challengers to the film company, four of which were manual versions with the larger, 440 cubic inch engine. No special modifications were made for filming, save that one car was equipped with heavy duty shock absorbers.

*Vanishing Point* has attained cult status, and not only with fans of snarling, snorting American pony cars. It works on more than one level, but if you're in the mood for a good, old-fashioned, non-CGI action movie then it more than satisfies on that level alone.

It was remade as a TV movie in 1997. It too features the Challenger R/T, but my advice would be to stick to the 1971 original.

# F15

*In the film 'The Blues Brothers', what car is used by Jake and Elwood Blues?*

**A.     Dodge Monaco**

Given their prodigious talent for getting into trouble with the law, it's entirely understandable that Elwood and Jake Blues required a car that was both fast and robust. Step forward a 1974 Dodge Monaco, an ex-police car with a 440 cubic inch engine and police-spec upgrades.

But whilst a 440 cubic inch (7.2 litre) V8 engine might give the impression of having power in abundance, this was far from the case for units manufactured after 1972. The need to meet strict US emissions targets meant that a post-1972 *440* had just 220 bhp on tap. Consequently, the heavy (4500 pounds) Monaco was far from being anyone's idea of a performance car, though one imagines that the ex-police car used by Jake and Elwood had been souped-up a little by its former owners.

Thirteen Dodge Monacos were used in filming. They and the other cars that appeared in the film had a hard life on set. Indeed, the film set a new record for the number of cars destroyed on-screen.

More impressive, however, was the destruction wrought during a chase scene in a shopping mall. Unlike modern films, the option to film the sequence using CGI simply didn't exist in 1980. That being so, the film company shot the scenes in the Dixie Square Mall in Harvey, Illinois, which had closed the year before filming took place. Although still in good condition when filming took place, the mall never re-opened. Instead, it became a dangerous and ever more dilapidated place until it was finally demolished in 2012.

The fate of the Monacos used in the film is less clear. Many replicas have been built over the years, with varying degrees of accuracy, but it's claimed that one original remains and is owned by the brother-in-law of actor Dan Aykroyd, who played Elwood Blues in the film.

A sequel, Blues Brothers 2000, was made in 1998. It featured a new

Bluesmobile, a 1990 Ford LTD Crown Victoria, and broke its predecessor's record for the number of cars wrecked on-screen.

## F16

*What car was featured in the 1967 film, 'The Graduate'?*

**B.     Alfa Romeo 1600 Spider**

Forget Dustin Hoffman, Anne Bancroft, Katharine Ross and Simon & Garfunkel's theme song, *Mrs. Robinson*, the real star of *The Graduate* is the Alfa Romeo Spider driven vigorously by Hoffman's character as the film reaches its climax.

Launched in 1966, the Spider's twin-cam 1570cc engine produced a more than respectable 109 bhp that, coupled with a kerb weight of under a tonne, endowed it with sprightly performance and a raspy soundtrack.

Given its role in a hit film, it would be reasonable to assume that queues, orderly or otherwise, formed outside Alfa Romeo dealerships. That this didn't happen was down largely to the high price tag which the Spider carried: in the USA it cost more than a Lotus Elan, and in the UK it was only a little cheaper than a Jaguar E-type.

The Spider was revised and upgraded over the years: it gained a 1779cc engine in 1967; some models were fitted with mechanical fuel-injection in 1969; and it lost its distinctive rounded tail with the launch of the series 2 model in 1970. A 2.0 litre engine appeared in 1971 and, to the horror of many, its chromed steel bumpers were replaced by unattractive impact-absorbing rubber bumpers in 1975, a move that was necessary to comply with US legislation.

The Spider nonetheless soldiered on into the 1980s. A series three version was introduced in 1982, and in the USA a *Graduate* model, which featured a more basic trim level as per the 1966 Spider, appeared. A final version, the series 4, was launched in 1990. Bedecked in a plastic bodykit that included somewhat boxy sill extensions, this version moved even further away from the delicacy of the 1960s original.

Production ended in 1993, with just over 124,000 examples having been built in the model's twenty-seven year production life.

## F17

*What car does the character played by Dennis Weaver drive in the film 'Duel'?*

**D.     Plymouth Valiant**

Steven Spielberg's directorial debut, *Duel,* is a tense, taut thriller with the simplest of premises: David Mann (Weaver) is a somewhat put-upon, middle-aged businessman driving through the Mojave Desert to meet a client. En route, he becomes embroiled in a fight for survival against a rusty tanker driven by an unseen man. And that's pretty much it.

Choosing the right car for Mann to drive was extremely important. It had to fit his character and circumstances to a tee, so it had to be an American car that wasn't too sporty, too luxurious (no electric windows) or too old. And while it couldn't be too gaudy, it did have to be red in order to stand out against the desert background.

Step forward the Plymouth Valiant, a capable but unexciting compact car that fitted Mann to a tee. Although *Duel* was made for TV and therefore on a limited budget, three Valiants were used in filming: a 1970 model with a 318 cubic inch V8 engine and two slightly later six-cylinder Valiants, both with the 225 cubic inch Slant-6 unit.

*Duel* aired on 13th November 1971 as part of ABC's *Movie of the Week* series and an extended version was later released in cinemas.

## F18

*In the TV series 'Return of the Saint', what car does the titular character drive?*

**A.     Jaguar XJ-S**

Were it not for the reluctance of its manufacturers to supply an E-Type to the producers of *The Saint*, Simon Templar (a.k.a. The Saint) would have had a Jaguar rather than a Volvo P1800 as his on-screen mode of transport in 1962 instead of having to wait until 1978.

Nine years after the end of the original series, in which Roger Moore played Simon Templar, the series was re-born, with Ian Ogilvy playing the debonair crime-fighter. Jaguar came on board this time around, supplying a white XJ-S to the show's producers, ITC.

The car supplied by Jaguar was a two year old XJ-S with a four-speed manual gearbox (rarely found on the V12 models) and sunroof. It had been used as a test car prior to being loaned to ITC.

Although the manual XJ-S (which still exists) appeared in most of the 24 episodes filmed, two other cars (loaned by Jaguar dealers) were also used. Neither was identical to the main XJ-S, with both having automatic gearboxes and one having a black rather than tan interior. So next time you watch an episode of *Return of the Saint*, why not see if you can tell whether the car being used is the manual XJ-S or one of the two stand-ins.

### F19

*In the 1975 James Bond film, 'The Man With The Golden Gun', what car performs a 270 degree roll whilst jumping over a river?*

**A.    AMC Hornet X**

Roger Moore's second outing as James Bond was an enjoyable romp, not least because of a sequence involving a car with nothing below it but air.

In fact, there were two such scenes in the film. In one of them, the villain of the piece literally takes off in an AMC Matador kitted out with wings and a propeller. Alas, the car which took to the air was a model; the real thing stayed resolutely on terra firma.

However, the scene in which Bond's AMC Hornet X takes off from one end of a ruined bridge, performs a barrel roll as it traverses a river and then lands safely on the other end of the bridge was the real thing.

You probably know that already, but did you know that the stunt had first been performed two years previously at the Houston Astrodome?

The story goes that Robert McHenry, the author of a computer programme designed to model vehicle crashes, came up with the idea for a new type of stunt that would help to showcase the abilities of his programme. Accordingly, he contacted Jay Milligan, the owner of an automotive stunt show, and suggested that the two work together on the stunt, each using their respective talents.

The stunt they came up with was the Astro-Spiral, a jump between two ramps in which the vehicle making the jump would rotate in flight. Armed with McHenry's calculations, Milligan built a specially adapted AMC Javelin – AMC provided the vehicles for his show – and used it to perform the Astro-Spiral at the Houston Astrodome in January 1972.

It was a short leap (if you'll excuse the pun) from there to landing a deal to perform the stunt in the next James Bond film.

As the Javelin had meantime gone out of production, the Hornet X was selected to perform the stunt. Milligan modified it extensively: the engine was repositioned behind the front axle, a roll cage and reinforced suspension were fitted and the steering wheel was moved to a central position. By the time Milligan had finished, little more than the Hornet's original body panels and engine remained.

Two such cars were shipped out to Thailand for filming. Although Milligan was on set as the stunt coordinator, it was stuntman Loren 'Bumps' Willert who successfully performed the jump, and at the first time of asking.

**F20**

*What car, then owned by George Harrison, appears in the video for The Beatles' 1996 single, 'Real Love'?*

**B.      Mercedes 500 SEL AMG**

George Harrison loved cars. And being a Beatle, he had the funds available to indulge in his passion. Over the years he owned a host of highly desirable cars, including an Aston Martin DB5, a Jaguar E-Type, a Porsche 928 S, several Ferraris (including a 275 GTB and 330 GTC), and a McLaren F1.

But the car we're concerned with is a black Mercedes-Benz 500 SEL AMG that he purchased new in 1984 and kept for sixteen years, covering over 30,000 miles in it.

In 1996, it made a brief appearance in the video for the Beatles 'new' single, *Real Love,* in which all three of the then surviving Beatles could be seen to exit it. But impressive though that is, one of Harrison's other cars – a customised Mini Cooper with a psychedelic paint job - appeared in the Beatles' film, *Magical Mystery Tour*. Moreover, that particular Mini also has the distinction of having been owned by another British musical icon, Eric Clapton.

The Mercedes is still on the road and has appeared at auction a couple of times in the last few years, fetching just over £43,000 in 2018. George Harrison's Mini has also survived to the present day. Whoever owns it is sitting on a small fortune - Paul McCartney's identical (save for the paint job) Mini Cooper made £182,000 at auction in 2018, which makes the Mercedes seem like a bit of a bargain.

# General Knowledge VII

## G61

*On what car was the Fiat Barchetta based?*

**A.     Fiat Punto**

There was a time when Fiat's model range invariably contained several roadsters – correction, several pretty and sweet-driving roadsters.

But then they started to disappear.

1973 saw the end of both the gorgeous, Ferrari V6-powered Fiat Dino Spider and the cute 850 Spider, their exits made a little less painful by the launch of the X1/9 the preceding year.

Another double retirement came in 1982, when Fiat ceased to build both the venerable 124 Sport Spider and the X1/9, albeit their respective builders, Pininfarina and Bertone, took over production of them. Fiat did not replace either car, both of which carried on for a little while longer in their new guises: the 124 finally departing in 1985 and the X1/9 four years later.

Now there were no Fiat roadsters, not even ones wearing the badge of another marque.

In 1995, however, Fiat unveiled a new roadster, the Barchetta. It was small, pretty and had front-wheel drive, courtesy of its Fiat Punto underpinnings.

The Barchetta quickly proved that it was more than just a pretty face. It handled well, had a surprisingly roomy cabin (having front-wheel drive obviated the need for a transmission tunnel) and its 1747cc DOHC engine gave it enough performance (124mph, 0-60mph in 8.6 seconds) to at least match its main rival, the Mazda MX-5.

Fiat only 'officially' sold 751 Barchettas in the UK, partly because it was only ever built in left-hand drive form, but also because astute buyers found that it was possible to import a new Barchetta from continental Europe for a much more attractive price than a UK Fiat dealer could offer. As these personal imports were not included in Fiat's official UK sales figures, the actual number of Barchettas which found their way to these shores is rather higher than the figure mentioned above.

As with the X1/9, Fiat didn't do much to develop the Barchetta over its eleven year lifespan, although it did receive a modest facelift in 2003.

Production ceased in 2005, and it would be a decade before Fiat once again returned to the roadster sector.

## G62

*What colour was the Ford Mustang Steve McQueen drove in the film 'Bullitt'?*

**C.    Highland Green**

If nothing else, *Bullitt* utterly redefined the cinematic car chase.

It was brilliantly shot and edited (we can forgive the fact that the same green VW Beetle appears several times during the chase), was perfectly paced, made excellent use of sound and, of course, it featured a Ford Mustang GT 390.

Truth be told, though, the Dodge Charger R/T than McQueen chases through the streets of San Francisco was much the quicker car, having an extra 50bhp to its name. The Mustang looks cooler, though, with or without Steve McQueen at the helm.

The film's quest for realism meant that both the Mustang and the Charger were very close to production specification, save for having uprated suspension in order to cope with the pounding they would take during the sequences filmed on the hills of San Francisco.

Two Mustangs were used for the close-up and action sequences.

However, as only one of them came with the GT pack, the grilles and badging of both cars were removed in order to harmonise their appearances. Even so, sharp-eyed Mustang fans can still tell which version was used in some scenes.

Reality is a key element of the car chase in *Bullitt* - you won't find a supercar struggling to outpace a shopping hack in this film. With that in mind, Steve McQueen wanted to do the stunt driving. In the end, though, it was Bud Ekins (who performed the iconic motorcycle jump in *The Great Escape*) who did much of the stunt driving in the Mustang. There was no need to strap another driver into the Charger for the stunt scenes, however, as legendary stunt driver Bill Hickman played its driver in the film and drove it in the chase sequences.

The third human star of the car chase scenes (four, if you count McQueen, who did some of the driving) was Pat Hustis, the builder and driver of the camera car used to film some of the later chase scenes.

Between the drivers, Carey Lofton (who designed the chase sequences) and the film crew, they produced a car chase that remains the gold standard for authenticity more than half a century after it was filmed, even if the climactic scene didn't quite work out as intended...

Oh, and if you're wondering about the colour, Highland Green was only available on 1968 model year Mustangs.

## G63

*What was the name of the notchback three-box saloon version of the Lancia Beta?*

**B.     Trevi**

Launched in 1972, the Lancia Beta was offered in a variety of guises over the years. The Berlina (a fastback saloon) was followed by the short-wheelbase coupé in 1973, the Spyder, a convertible with 2+2 seating, followed in 1974, and the High Performance Estate shooting brake appeared in 1975. And just for good measure, the Beta name was added as a prefix to the first series of the company's new Montecarlo sports car, launched in 1976.

With one exception (which we'll get to), every model of the Beta range had looks on its side. They drove well too, with fine performance and handling. But there were two problems, one of which almost destroyed Lancia's reputation.

The first issue was with its running gear. To some purists, the Beta's use of Fiat-derived engines meant that it wasn't a proper Lancia, and it mattered not that those engines were advanced, well-engineered DOHC units designed by Aurelio Lampredi.

But that was a minor issue. The second was, however, much more damning: corrosion. Early Betas, in particular, acquired a reputation for rusting away with great alacrity. Some commentators have blamed the Beta's rust problems on poor quality steel supplied by the Soviet Union, but that's an urban myth. The reality is more prosaic: like many cars of its era, the Beta suffered from poor build quality and woefully inadequate rustproofing. In the UK, the situation got so bad that Lancia offered to buy back Betas, a move that cost them plenty of money but did nothing to improve the reputation of their products.

Which brings us to the Trevi. Introduced in 1980 as the Beta Trevi, the Trevi was a traditional three-box saloon that featured a curious dashboard with more holes than a Swiss cheese. Dashboard aside, the Trevi's looks were, to put it politely, challenging. Still, Lancia hoped that it would help to restore the company's credibility.

Like all Betas, the Trevi was a good car to drive, but that wasn't ever going to be enough to win back public confidence. A change of name followed in 1983, when it became known simply as the Lancia Trevi. In retrospect, Lancia should have called it that from the beginning rather than burdening it with the Beta prefix and all that came with it.

Production ceased in 1984, with 36,784 examples having been built.

### G64

*What engine was used to power Bill Collins's original DeLorean DMC-*

*12 prototype?*

## C. Citroën 2.2 litre

One of the first people to join John DeLorean's fledgling car company was Bill Collins. Having spent 16 years at Pontiac, where he'd worked with DeLorean on the GTO, Collins was headhunted by his former colleague in 1974, thereby becoming DeLorean Motor Corporation's chief engineer.

The project was very much in its infancy when Collins joined the team. At that early stage, DeLorean's concept amounted to little more than a wish list: attractive lines, gullwing doors, advanced safety features, and strong performance allied to good fuel economy. The car's structure was also to make innovative use of plastics, DeLorean having obtained a licence to use a process known as Elastic Reservoir Moulding ('ERM').

Collins thereafter played a key role in every aspect of the design and construction of the prototype, from working out its dimensions to liaising with the car's stylist, Giorgetto Giugiaro, and the sub-contractors who built it to DMC's specifications.

Although of similar appearance to the production car, there were more differences than similarities between the two. For example, the handbuilt prototype lacked the Lotus-engineered backbone chassis of the production vehicles, the style and function of the prototype's side windows differed greatly from that of the production cars, and the prototype lacked the later car's rear louvre.

The engine differed too. As the prototype was a running development model rather than a static show car, it needed to have an engine. But instead of the Renault-supplied 2664cc V6 engine found on production models, the prototype used a 2.2 litre Citroën engine.

The prototype was completed in 1976, with DeLorean optimistically claiming that it would go into production in 1978. However, the need to raise the money to productionise and build it meant that it would be 1981 before it finally went on sale. Not much of Collins's work remained by then, as Lotus, who engineered the car for production under contract to DeLorean, made radical changes in order to get it production-ready in a short space of time. Out went ERM, and in came VARI and Lotus's signature Y-shaped backbone chassis. Indeed, the car that finally emerged had more in common with a Lotus Esprit than Collins's prototype.

As for Bill Collins, he parted company with DeLorean in 1979, frustrated that he was being frozen out of the process of turning his prototype into a production car.

## G65

*Which actress provided the voice used by the 'talking dashboard' of the early MG and Vanden Plas models of the Austin Maestro?*

**B.     Nicolette McKenzie**

An honest appraisal of the Austin Maestro might be expected to contain the following words and phrases: "worthy", "comfortable", and "a bit dull".

Back in the early 1980s, one wonders if BL knew that their forthcoming Austin Maestro was, well, worthy enough but a bit dull*. If so, it might explain their decision to jazz up the the MG and Vanden Plas models by fitting them not only with digital instruments but also with a system whereby a politely-spoken lady apprised anyone within earshot of important information such as "Warning – low oil pressure", "Have the washer fluid topped up", and "You're not going out with that shirt on, are you?" Okay, I made up the last one but you get the picture.

The politely spoken lady in question was Nicolette McKenzie, a New Zealand actress who had appeared in several UK TV series.

In spite of the dulcet tones with which it had been endowed, the 'talking dashboard' was not popular with owners, not least because it was a bit of a chatterbox in early cars. Consequently, it was dropped in 1986, at which time the digital display was also replaced by conventional analogue instruments.

* Under no circumstances could the later MG Maestro Turbo ever be called dull!

## G66

*The cheapest version of the TVR Tasmin was powered by which four-cylinder engine?*

**A.    Ford 2.0 litre 'Pinto'**

The TVR 'wedges' of the 1980s were all hairy chested, road-burning monsters powered by rumbling V8 engines, weren't they?

Er, no. Not all of them. Some came with six and others even had, whisper it, *four* cylinders.

At launch in 1980, the wedge had a name, *Tasmin,* and came with a 2.8 litre version of Ford's *Cologne* V6 engine. It was joined a year later by a 2.0 litre version, powered by Ford's *Pinto* engine. And that, for a time, was that – there was nary a V8 to be seen nor heard.

The Tasmin 200, as the Pinto-engined version was called, was offered as a cheaper route into TVR ownership. But with only 101bhp on tap, its claimed top speed of 115mph and modest acceleration (0 to 60mph took 9.6 seconds) failed to set pulses racing. Consequently, it sold poorly and only 61 examples (45 convertibles and 16 coupés) were built before it was dropped in 1983.

That same year saw the launch of the first V8 version, the Tasmin 350i, equipped with the trusty 3.5 litre Rover V8. The Ford V6-powered Tasmin 280i remained in production until 1988, but the Tasmin name was dropped in 1984.

## G67

*The Alfa Romeo SZ was given which nickname in Italy?*

**C.    Il Mostro**

There are mean-looking cars and then there's the Alfa Romeo SZ, a coupé that looks for all the world like someone's spilled its drink. Little wonder, then, that Italians called it 'the monster'.

Based on an Alfa 75 platform, the SZ's pugnacious shape is largely the product of Alfa's in-house styling office and CAD systems, although it wears Zagato's stylised 'Z' badge on its flanks.

Powered by a 3.0 litre version of Alfa's celebrated *Busso* V6 engine, the SZ featured some cutting-edge technology in its day, including the use of composites, aluminium and steel in its construction as well as dampers that could be adjusted for height using a button on the dashboard.

Accommodation is limited to a driver and passenger and whatever they could fit into the space behind the seats; the SZ has a boot but you'd struggle to fit anything bigger than a toothbrush into it.

But who cares about luggage space. The real question is: how does it go? Pretty well, as it happens. It's not blazingly fast in a straight line (147mph, 0-60mph in 7 seconds) but the *Busso* delivers a glorious soundtrack.

As for handling, it's fair to say that in the dry the SZ has more grip than a politician holding an expenses cheque. It can be quite unruly in the wet, though, with oversteer being apt to appear whether demanded or not. And just to make matters a little more sporty, there's no ABS or traction control: **you** drive the SZ.

There were no factory right-hand drive cars nor could you buy one in any other colour except red. But if that didn't suit you then there was always the SZ's convertible sibling, the RZ.

### G68

*What vehicle formed the basis of the 'Popemobile' used during the Papal visit to Spain in 1982?*

**D.**     **SEAT Panda**

There was an element of both the sublime and the ridiculous in so far as the vehicles used by Pope John Paul II in his 1982 visits to Great Britain and Spain was concerned.

Just days before the Pope's visit to Spain, it was discovered that the vehicle in which he was to be conveyed was too wide to pass through the doors of the Camp Nou and Bernabéu stadiums, where the main events of his visit were to take place. SEAT therefore quickly designed and produced an alternative vehicle, an open-topped, glassless (save for the windscreen) vehicle based on a SEAT Panda.

For his visit to Britain, however, a heavily modified* Leyland Constructor truck, with bullet-proof glass and armour plating, was used.

Both vehicles still exist. The Panda is part of SEAT's heritage collection and the Constructor truck is on display at the British Commercial Vehicle Museum in Leyland.

* By Ogle Design.

### G69

*Lotus Elan designer Ron Hickman also designed which famous product?*

**B.     Black & Decker WorkMate**

That Ron Hickman failed to become a household name might just be one of life's enduring mysteries. After all, how many people can claim to have designed the definitive sports car of its era, the Lotus Elan, and an ingenious device, the WorkMate, that has sold over 100 million units and become the best friend of many a DIYer.

Born in South Africa, Hickman worked for Ford in the UK before moving to Lotus, then in its infancy. At Lotus, he worked on the Elite but played a much more significant role in designing the road car that made the marque's name, the Elan. He followed this up by working on the Elan+2 and Europa models prior to his departure from Lotus in 1967.

He thereafter worked for Cunard on the design of the QE2's lounge seating as well as on a personal project, a portable workbench that came to be known as the WorkMate.

In spite of the obvious utility of his portable workbench, Hickman had some difficulty in finding a company willing to put it into mass production. Finally, however, a deal was struck with Black & Decker and the WorkMate went into production in 1973. It was hugely successful and made Hickman a wealthy man.

He moved to Jersey in 1977, where he designed his own house and, ever creative, filled it with his inventions.

He passed away in 2011.

## G70

*Which British car was sold in Italy as the Innocenti Regent?*

**A.     Austin Allegro**

A British car built in Italy in the 1970s; what could possibly go wrong?

Italian manufacturer Innocenti had enjoyed a close relationship with BL's predecessors, BMC and BLMC, in the 1960s, building a number of vehicles, including the Mini and the Austin-Healey Sprite (marketed as the Innocenti Spider in Italy), under licence.

Sales were reasonably strong, and in 1972 BL purchased Innocenti. Two years later, Innocenti commenced production of the Austin Allegro. The name given to the resulting car, the Innocenti Regent, wasn't the only difference between it and UK-made Allegros: the Regent had front quarterlights, a different grille, and distinct seats and instruments.

Two engines were offered: a 1.3 litre A-series and a 1.5 litre E-series and there were two trim levels.

Unfortunately, the Regent failed to win over Italian buyers, and production ended after only 18 months, with just over 11,000 Regents having been built.

In the same year as Regent production started, Innocenti introduced a rebodied Mini. In this new, Bertone-styled guise, the Mini acquired an attractive, bang up-to-date, hatchback body. It was so well received that BL considered making it available in the UK. However, BL's financial woes and consequent nationalisation put paid to that idea.

Although Innocenti was sold to De Tomaso in 1976, production of its hatchback Mini continued. It gained Diahatsu power in the early 1980s and remained in production until 1993. It was not, however, ever officially imported to the UK.

# It's a Numbers Game II

## N11

*In what year was the MGB first sold in the UK with rubber rather than chrome bumpers?*

**B.    1974**

The switch from dainty chrome to substantial rubber bumpers has long been a sore point with MG enthusiasts, but there was a good reason behind it, at least in so far as US-market cars were concerned.

That reason was the need to comply with legislation introduced in the USA, MG's biggest market, by the National Highway Traffic Safety Administration. This stipulated that all new cars sold in the US must be equipped with front and rear bumpers that could sustain a 5 mile per hour impact without any damage resulting to the car's lights, engine and safety equipment.

The result was fitment of chunky black bumpers to the MG B, B GT and Midget and the consequent raising of the ride height, the latter doing the cars' handling no favours.

## N12

*How many examples of the Citroën GS Birotor were built?*

**A.    847**

As a manufacturer who prided itself on forward-thinking, it was inevitable that Citroën would embrace rotary engine technology. Accordingly, it entered into a joint venture with NSU to develop and build rotary engines, engaged in mass public testing using a fleet of experimental road cars and, finally, in 1973 launched its first production rotary-engined car, the GS Birotor, also known as the GZ.

The Birotor's specification was highly impressive: twin-rotor engine with semi-automatic transmission, all-round disc brakes and hydropneumatic suspension. However, it shared relatively few components with other models in the GS range, with its hubs, floorpan, brakes, wheels, instrument panel, interior trim and even some of its exterior panels being unique to it.

Needless to say, this level of sophistication and individuality came at a price: the Birotor was 70% more expensive than any other GS. And although its 107bhp meant that it was easily the most powerful model in the GS range, it was also by far the thirstiest, poor fuel economy being one of the rotary engine's weaknesses. In normal times, that may not have mattered so much, but the global energy crisis that followed the 1973 Yom Kippur War significantly reduced the sales appeal of less fuel-efficient cars.

The Birotor might have survived that crisis, but other factors combined to bring about its demise. Confidence in rotary engines had been seriously damaged by the premature engine wear that had blighted the NSU Ro80. It mattered little that lessons learned from that debacle had ensured that the Birotor was much less susceptible to the same problems; it was guilty by association.

That was bad enough, but Citroën's financial situation was the clincher. By setting up the Comotor company with NSU, Citroën had hoped to gain an early lead in what was expected to be a burgeoning market for rotary engines. But as their weaknesses became understood, the motor industry shied away from them. Consequenly, Citroën's investment in Comotor would not be recovered. Moreover, the company had invested heavily in new cars, the GS and the CX, and by 1974, its finances were in a parlous state.

The outcome of this was a takeover by Peugeot and the implementation of severe cost-cutting measures. The Birotor was one of the casualties of this programme. Production ceased in 1975, and Citroën then attempted to buy back every Birotor it had sold, reasoning that it was cheaper to do so than manufacture and stock spare parts for a car sold in such low volumes. The terms of the buy-back offer were generous and many Birotors thus found their way back to Citroën, where they were unceremoniously scrapped.

Not all of the 847 Birotors built perished in the cull, however, and an unknown number survive to this day.

## N13

*|In what year did the Ford Cortina mark IV go on sale in in the UK?*

**A.    1976**

First launched in 1962, the Ford Cortina was built in four different generations (the mark V was little more than a facelifted mark IV) over a twenty year period. It sold in huge numbers and was popular with both fleet buyers and private owners.

The Cortina was a car that evolved through a series of small changes rather than through periodic revolution. When it started, its competitors shared its three-box saloon shape and rear-wheel drive configuration, but as time passed an ever-growing number of them evolved into front-wheel drive hatchbacks. The Cortina did not.

There was a time in the 1960s when the Cortina was able to bask in the achievements of the racing and rally versions, but this was very much a thing of the past by the time that the mark IV appeared in 1976. Moreover, there was nothing about the Cortina that could be described as cutting-edge. Rather, it appealed as a solid, relatively simple car that was reliable, affordable to run, enjoyable to drive and had the backing of a huge service network.

Ford had adopted a pragmatic approach to the design of the mark IV, concentrating on making a number of relatively minor but effective improvements rather than starting with a clean sheet. The styling of the mark IV was sharper and more modern than its predecessor whilst its cabin was lighter and airier. Otherwise, it was much as it had been before, with the mark III's tried and trusted running gear being retained.

As expected, the mark IV followed its predecessor's example and went straight to the top of the sales charts and stayed there for the remainder of the 1970s.

## N14

*In which year did it become compulsory in the UK for a front seat occupant of a car to wear a seat belt?*

**B.**   **1983**

In 1968, a law came into effect that required the fitment of three-point front seat belts to all new cars. It also stipulated that seat belts had to be retroactively fitted to all cars manufactured between 1965 and 1968, earlier legislation having required such cars to be fitted with seat belt anchorage points.

Over a decade of inaction followed, and it wasn't until the Motor Vehicles (Wearing of Seat Belts) Regulations 1982 came into effect on 31 January 1983 that front seat occupants of cars* were required to wear a seat belt.

There were, of course, certain exemptions to this, one of which applied to the front seat occupants of pre-1965 cars not fitted with seat belts.

There was, in addition, a loophole in the legislation that, for a time, meant that the requirement to wear a seat belt did **not** apply to the occupier of the *middle* seat of two post-1965 cars - the Matra-Simca Bagheera and Talbot-Matra Murena, both of which had three-abreast seating - **if** the passenger's seat (i.e. the one next to the passenger door) was occupied by another person.

For some reason, however, another eight years passed before rear-seat passengers were obliged to buckle up.

\* The legislation applied to more than just cars.

## N15

*How many Vauxhall Belmonts were licensed in the UK as at the second quarter of 2020?*

**C.**   **17**

Introduced in 1986 as a saloon version of the mark 2 Vauxhall Astra, the Belmont's large boot gave it both excellent luggage capacity and a somewhat ungainly appearance.

The Belmont range was conservative in comparison to the Astra. There was, for example, no GTE model; the 122bhp SRi being the nearest thing to a sporty Belmont. This was because the Belmont was expected to appeal to older people who preferred traditional saloon cars to hatchbacks and, as such, were thought to be much less likely to find a rorty, body-kitted, wide-tyred model to their taste.

As it turned out, the Belmont didn't attract anything like as many buyers as its hatchback sibling, with only around 50,000 being sold between 1986 and the end of production in 1991. That marked the end of the line for the Belmont name, as it was not carried over to the mark 3 Astra.

The Belmont did, however, attain notoriety more than a decade later when it became proportionately the most commonly stolen car in the UK.

Today, it's very much an endangered species, with only 17 examples having been licensed in the UK as at the second quarter of 2020. A further 75 Belmonts are SORNd, but it's unclear as to how many, if any, will ever return to the road.

It's a sad picture, as although the Belmont may not have been the last word in, well, anything, it performed a valuable if unglamorous role for thousands of people up and down the land. For that reason alone, it surely deserves a better fate than the unlamented extinction for which it is seemingly headed.

## N16

*In what year did the Fiat X1/9 become the Bertone X1/9?*

**A.**     **1982**

If you include the concept car on which it was based, the Autobianchi A112 Runabout, the Fiat X1/9 wore the insignia of three different marques during its time.

As the 1960s came to a close, Fiat was readying a new small saloon for launch, the front-wheel drive 128. The new car would have a new engine too, a four-cylinder SOHC engine designed by Aurelio Lampredi.

In those days, Fiat had a habit of producing a sporty, convertible version of its saloons. An open-top version of the 128 therefore seemed to be very much on the cards. There was, however, some concern that the USA, an important export market for Fiat soft-tops, intended to impose rollover safety requirements that would effectively outlaw traditional convertibles.

The obvious solution was therefore to build a car that had the rollover protection of a saloon but most of the freedom afforded by a convertible. Or, in other words, a car with a detachable roof.

The result was the X1/9. Inspired by Bertone's Autobianchi A112 Runabout prototype of 1969, the X1/9 shared its 1290cc engine and gearbox with the Fiat 128 but that's where the similarities ended, for whereas the 128 was front-engined and had front-wheel drive, the X1/9s engine was mounted amidships and drove the rear wheels.

At launch in 1972, the X1/9's Gandini-penned lines caused a sensation; it had the style and poise of a Ferrari without the price tag, and its mid-engined layout meant that it handled like one too.

It wasn't especially fast but its good fuel consumption was an asset, particularly during the global energy crisis of 1973/4. There was, however, one problem in so far as UK buyers were concerned: it was only available in left-hand drive form until 1976, save for a few examples converted to RHD by Radbourne Racing.

Fiat didn't do much to develop the X1/9, save for a few detail changes, the fitting of more substantial bumpers (those on post-1975 US models being unattractive but necessary to meet new US regulations), and the replacement in 1979 of the 1.3 litre engine with a 1.5 litre unit, which raised power from 75bhp to 85bhp.

The X1/9s bodyshell had been built by Bertone from the get-go, with the cars thereafter being transported to Fiat for completion. By 1982, however, the X1/9 had been on the market for a decade with precious little development. And with Fiat about to withdraw from the US market, the writing seemed to be on the wall for the X1/9.

Bertone was, however, keen to continue to produce the X1/9. Consequently, a deal was struck whereby the X1/9 became a Bertone product, with Fiat supplying the running gear and other components.

The first Bertone-badged X1/9s appeared in 1982 for the 1983 model year. Although Fiat had now ceased operations Stateside, the X1/9 continued to be sold in the key US market, initially via International Automobile Importers, Inc. and latterly by M.I.K. Automotive Inc.

Production of the X1/9 finally ended in 1989 after 160,000 examples had been built, of which 19,500 were the later Bertone-badged models.

## N17

*In January 1977 a Lotus Esprit cost £8051 on the road. How much did the corresponding model cost in June 1981.*

**B.    £13,513**

Okay, the 1977 price is for an Esprit S1 and the one from 1981 is for an S3*, but as both were the entry level Esprit in their respective days (the only Esprit in the case of the S1) it's a fair comparison.

The reason for the leap in price was due to that most 1970s of bogeymen: inflation. It may seem hard to believe now, but the rate of inflation in the UK was 24.2% in 1975 and remained above 10% in five of the six years that followed.

And it wasn't just expensive, high-performance cars that saw their prices jump. For example, in January 1977 you could buy a Citroën CX 2200 Diesel for £4699. Fast forward to May 1981 and you'd need to find £8639 to take home the corresponding 25D model. Likewise, you could buy a brand new Renault 14TL for £2699 in June, 1977. By May 1981, however, the price had shot up to £4096.

*In spite of the substantial price hike between 1977 to 1981, the Esprit S3's launch price of £13,513 was actually £1700 cheaper than the S2.2 model it replaced in April 1981.

**N18**

*In what year was the Triumph name last used on a new car?*

**B.     1984**

Having started out life in the 1880s as an importer then maker of bicycles, Triumph's first foray into production of motorised vehicles was as a manufacturer of motorcycles.

In 1923, Triumph produced its first car, the 10/20, which was designed for it by another British motor manufacturer, Lea-Francis. The company's first truly successful model, the Super 7, followed in 1927 but the economic recession of the 1930s saw the company hit hard times. The bicycle and motorcycle production arms of the business were sold in 1936, and although Triumph struggled on for a while, it went into receivership in 1939.

Its assets were purchased by a scrap metal company, Thomas W. Ward Ltd., and Donald Healey was installed as General Manager. However, the advent of the Second World War brought car production to a halt. And to make matters worse, the company's factory was thereafter heavily damaged in a bombing rate.

The Standard Motor Company bought the remnants of the Triumph Motor Company in 1944, by which time pretty much all that remained was a bombed-out factory, the Triumph name and the goodwill.

Production of a new range of Triumphs began in 1946 but the company, now known as Standard-Triumph, was taken over by Leyland Motors in 1960. This marked the beginning of Triumph's greatest era, one in which it offered a series of saloons with a sporting bent as well as out and out sports cars.

In 1968, Leyland merged with the British Motor Corporation and became British Leyland Motor Corporation. Although new models continued to appear up to the mid-1970s, British Leyland was struggling to maintain its market share and was nationalised in 1975. No all-new Triumphs appeared after that and the existing models were gradually phased out.

By 1981 only the TR7 remained in production, but it would not see out the year. A final Triumph-badged car appeared that same year, the Acclaim. This, however, was little more than a badge-engineered Honda Ballade which British Leyland built under licence.

The Acclaim remained in production until 1984, when it was replaced by the new, Honda-based Rover 200 series.

The rights to the Triumph name have been owned by BMW since the mid-1990s. It seems unlikely, however, that the marque will be making a comeback any time soon.

### N19

*In what year did the V12-powered Series 3 version of the Jaguar E-Type first go on sale in the UK?*

**D.     1971**

The Jaguar E-Type caused quite a stir when it was launched in 1961. Aside from its sleek lines, its speed and advanced specification, which included all-independent suspension and four-wheel disc brakes, set it apart from the competition.

A series of upgrades throughout the 1960s, which included the fitting of a larger, 4.2 litre six-cylinder engine and the introduction in 1966 of a 2+2 version of the coupé, ensured that it kept its place at the top table of desirable motor cars throughout that decade.

By 1971, however, the E-Type was a decade old. Time, then, for Jaguar to unveil one last big upgrade: a 5.3 litre V12 engine that offered relatively modest gains in power and torque but a considerable amount of extra cachet over the previous six-cylinder engines.

Every series 3 E-Type produced* was fitted with the V12 unit, though the 4.2 litre engine continued to provide sterling service in various Jaguars and Daimlers for another two decades.

*15,290 series 3 E-Types were produced from 1971 until the end of E-Type production in 1975.

## N20

*The Vignale-styled Fiat Samantha coupé was based on which model?*

**D.   125**

If you've never seen a Fiat Samantha then stop reading this, fire up the search engine of your choice and give your eyes a treat. And once you've done that, come back and read its story.

Based on the Fiat 125S, the Samantha was designed by Alfredo Vignale, the proprietor of the famous Turin-based styling house. The story goes that Vignale wanted a coupé that looked exotic but was practical and reliable enough to use as a daily driver, so he designed the Samantha around his own requirements.

Looking for all the world like a mini-supercar and with a luxurious interior, the Samantha was launched at the 1967 Turin Motor Show. Aimed at wealthy individuals, many of those built ended up in the hands of one man: Frixos Demetriou.

Demetriou was a Greek Cypriot who ran a successful casino in London. But with the gambling industry being something of a political hot potato in the second half of the 1960s, Demetriou decided to explore other commercial avenues.

A chance sighting of a Vignale Gamine, a cute open-top car based on the Fiat 500, on a business trip resulted in Demetriou making a bulk purchase of Vignale-built, Fiat-based cars, including the Samantha. As Demetriou intended to sell these cars in the UK, he arranged with Vignale that they be built in right-hand drive form.

Back in London, Demetriou wasted no time in exhibiting his purchases at the 1968 Earl's Court Motor Show. He followed this up by being featured – in long, dark coat and sunglasses – on the cover of the January 1969 issue of *Car* magazine.

There were, however, a few clouds on Demetriou's horizon. The cars were too expensive, with the 1.6 litre Samantha costing more than a Jaguar E-Type; servicing them caused a few headaches too, as although Fiat in Italy had agreed with Demetriou that Fiat UK would provide after-sales service, they'd omitted to inform Fiat UK of this; and just to put the icing on the cake, the build quality was decidedly iffy and the cars had a tendency to corrode quickly in the dank British climate.

Demetriou now found himself with several hundred unsold cars in the UK and no imminent prospect of shifting them. So having imported them to the UK, he now exported them...to Cyprus. From a sales point of view, it was a sensible move, with the Gamine in particular finding buyers much easier to come by in sunny Cyprus.

For Demetriou, however, the move to Cyprus ended in tragedy in 1970. The circumstances of his demise are a little unclear but it appears that he lost his life as a result of an accident involving a vehicle belonging to the British Army, which, then as now, occupied bases on the island.

In a bizarre twist of fate, Demetriou's death was preceded in 1969 by that of Alfredo Vignale, who also perished in an accident. Vignale's death came only a few months after selling his company to De Tomaso, a move that brought about the demise of the Samantha after only 100 or so had been built.

# General Knowledge VIII

### G71

*Why was production of the Lancia Beta Montecarlo stopped for two years?*

**C.    Its brakes were prone to locking-up**

The Lancia Beta Montecarlo had a curious existence.

Conceived as a big brother to the Fiat X1/9 (its original Fiat designation was X1/8, later changed to X1/20), the project was moved across to Fiat-owned Lancia. And it was as a Lancia that it was uncovered at the Geneva Motor Show in 1975, with the production version appearing in showrooms a year later.

There was much to like about the Beta Montecarlo: its Pininfarina-penned lines and mid-engined layout gave it the air of a supercar, and its 2.0 litre Aurelio Lampredi-designed DOHC engine gave it enough power to reach a top speed of almost 120 miles per hour and cover the 0 to 60mph dash in a whisker over 8 seconds. There were even two versions to choose from: a coupé with a traditional roof and a Spider version with a targa-style fabric roof that could be rolled up and stored between the B-pillars.

But there was a problem: only the front brakes were servo-assisted and, worse still, they were too heavily assisted. The Montecarlo soon developed a reputation for being a car in which it was easy - too easy – to lock the front brakes, particularly on wet or damp roads.

Lancia withdrew the car from sale in 1978 so that the issues could be rectified, but it was two years before the Montecarlo (now shorn of its 'Beta' prefix) returned to the showrooms. There were a few detail changes, and the brake problems had been solved by removing the servo-assistance and fitting larger discs and calipers, but nothing had been done to the car that explained its long absence from showrooms.

The Montecarlo's return was a short one. Production ended in 1981, after only 7798 models (including the US market version) had been built.

## G72

*A special edition of which car was produced to celebrate Italy's hosting of the 1990 football world cup?*

**D.     Fiat Panda**

The FIFA World Cup was held in Italy in 1990, so naturally the country's largest corporation, FIAT, became involved.

Apart from Fiat-owned Alfa Romeo becoming one of the tournament's official sponsors, FIAT took the opportunity to produce a special *Italia 90* version of the Panda.

Mechanically, there was nothing special about the *Italia 90* Panda; it was simply a standard Panda 750L with a 769cc FIRE engine that put a mere 34bhp at the driver's disposal. The rest of it was, however, a bit special.

You could have your *Italia 90* Panda in any colour you desired as long as it was white. Green and red pinstripes adorned each flank, with the tournament mascot, *Ciao*, and 'Italia 90' (in the prescribed font, of course) appearing at the base of each C-pillar.

*Ciao* put in another appearance on the tailgate, but it was the wheel trims that drew the most attention. These featured black and white polygons (specifically, white hexagons and black pentagons) arranged in such a way as to look like a football – a nice touch. For some reason, though, these wheel trims were restricted to Italian and UK models; other markets had to make do with plain white ones.

Inside, the seats, carpets, door cards and dash coverings were blue, Italy's national sporting colour, and all four seats featured a small embroidered *Ciao*.

It all came together to create a car with a happy ambience. Little wonder, then, that Bobby Moore was smiling in the promotional shots taken at Wembley for the *Italia 90* Panda.

It's believed that around 475 *Italia 90* Pandas were sold in the UK, with at least nine being known to have survived to the present day.

## G73

*What was the first hot hatchback?*

**B.     Simca 1100 TI**

Simca only ever made one hot hatchback, but it just so happened to be the first of the breed.

At launch in 1967, the Simca 1100 was very much the car of the moment. It not only had an advanced specification – front-wheel drive, independent suspension all-round, rack and pinion steering, transverse engine and space-efficient hatchback shape – but used that specification to deliver a winning combination of space, practicality and excellent road manners. And its price was good too.

One thing it didn't have, however, was sporting appeal. Indeed, in its first three years on sale no 1100 was able to offer a power output of greater than 56bhp. A more powerful model, the 1100 Special, finally appeared in 1970, but apart from its 74bhp engine there was little else to distinguish it from the rest of the range.

The same charge could not, however, be laid at the door of the 1100TI. Launched in 1973, its 1294cc engine produced 81 bhp, enough to take it to a maximum speed of just over 100mph and hit 60mph from rest in under 12 seconds. The engine wasn't the only thing about the TI to stand apart from the rest of the 1100 range - the brakes, suspension and clutch were all uprated too.

And that's not all. The 1100 TI also featured interior and exterior enhancements that effectively amounted to a tutorial on how to create a hot hatchback out of a 'cooking' model. The TI boasted a six-gauge instrument panel, a steering wheel with the 'TI' logo picked out in red, alloy wheels, black grille, extra front lights, discrete spoilers at both ends of the car, and external 'TI' badging with red highlights.

To cap it all, Simca's marketing was careful to ensure that sales brochures carried at least one action shot of a TI cornering. Granted, this would be standard fare just a few years hence, but in 1973 it stood out.

The TI was never sold in the UK, which goes some way to explaining why it's received so little recognition here.

It would be ludicrous to claim that the 1100 TI was a match for the Golf GTI, but it was still the first of its kind and deserves to be remembered as such.

## G74

*In which British Leyland factory was the Triumph TR7 **not** built?*

**B.    Longbridge**

Initially available only in coupé form, the TR7's main market was the USA, and that's where all the early cars went. Indeed, it didn't go on sale in the UK in May 1976, more than a year after it was launched in the USA.

All of the early TR7s were built at Triumph's Speke factory. However, a series of labour disputes at the plant culminated in a lengthy strike that began in October 1977, just as production of the 1978 model year TR7 was getting under way. Several months passed before the strike ended, but by then British Leyland had decided to close the plant.

Production of the TR7 ceased in May 1978, when the Speke plant closed, and resumed five months later at BL's Canley factory. The Canley-built TR7s came with a few small upgrades over those built at Speke, and their build quality was better too. Moreover, two important new TR7 variants came into being at Canley: the TR7 convertible in 1979 (the USA got it that year, everywhere else had to wait until 1980) and the Rover V8-engined TR8 that entered production in 1980.

The convertible looked as stylish as the coupé was awkward, and the TR8, produced solely in convertible form and only for the US market, delivered the performance and soundtrack that sports car buyers in the USA expected.

In the early autumn of 1980, production of the TR7 and TR8 was moved to Solihull. It was to be their final home, with both the TR7/TR8 and the Solihull factory being victims of a cost-cutting drive. Production ceased once more, this time for good, in October 1981.

## G75

*What car was the subject of the first chapter of Ralph Nader's book, 'Unsafe at Any Speed'?*

**C.    Chevrolet Corvair**

Launched in 1960, the Chevrolet Corvair bucked at least one American design trend: its air-cooled flat-six engine was rear-mounted. This, said its maker, had certain advantages, including better traction, more space in the passenger cabin and a lower silhouette.

That all seemed fine enough, but the pre-1965 model year Corvair had a weakness – its swing-axle rear-suspension - that would be sensationalised by consumer protection activist Ralph Nader in his 1965 book, *Unsafe at Any Speed.*

Nader focused on the Corvair's handling, averring that a cost-cutting decision not to fit a front anti-roll bar* resulted in it having an unruly rear end due to its swing-axle suspension. Indeed, he referred to the Corvair in the chapter heading as "The one car accident."

For the 1965 model year, Chevrolet fitted a front anti-roll bar to the Corvair, and they went even further the following year, replacing the swing axles with a new, fully independent suspension set-up.

The damage was done, however. Corvair sales nosedived in 1966 and never recovered thereafter. Ironically, later tests by Texas A&M University and the National Highway Traffic Safety Administration each concluded that the pre-1965 Corvair did not, in fact, have greater potential for loss of control than its competitors.

Production ended in 1969 after 1,835,170 examples had been built.

*In the absence of an front anti-roll bar, Chevrolet had mandated that the Corvair's rear tyres should be inflated to a considerably higher pressure than the front, this being a technique used by other cars with swing-axle rear suspension. As a 'fix', it was, of course, wholly reliant upon the Corvair's owner/driver ensuring that its tyre pressures were maintained at the prescribed settings.

## G76

*Which fashion designer created a 'designer edition' of the Matra-Simca Bagheera sports car?*

**C.   André Courrèges**

André Courrèges was a French fashion designer who came to prominence in the 1960s. Best known for being one of the inventors of the mini-skirt, Courrèges' designs were influenced by modernism and futurism. It therefore made perfect sense for Matra, with their aerospace background and cutting-edge ideas, to collaborate with him.

Their partnership resulted in a special edition of Matra's three-seat, mid-engined Bagheera sports car. Launched in 1974, the Bagheera Courrèges was mechanically identical to the standard car. Externally, it was also just like every other Bagheera, save for its alloy wheels, Satin White paintwork and silver Courrèges logo.

The changes to the interior were also cosmetic rather than fundamental, with the seats and headlining being white, and the dash, door cards, gearknob, carpets and pair of detachable, door-mounted, Courrèges-branded handbags all being tan. It was restrained and (mostly) tasteful, particularly when compared to some 'designer editions'.

The Bagheera Courrèges was a core part of the Bagheera range rather than a limited edition model, and it remained part of the range (albeit with tan seats this time) when Matra launched the series 2 Bagheera in 1976.

Sales were, however, sluggish and the Bagheera Courrèges was replaced by a new upmarket model, the Bagheera X, in 1977.

Courrèges thereafter turned his attention to the Matra Rancho, and a prototype Rancho Courrèges appeared in 1978. It was finished in white, with wood effect bumpers and side impact strips. The interior had white velour seats, a fishing rod, landing net and a door-mounted thermos flask.

It would have cut quite a dash on the King's Road but, alas, it never made it into production.

C'est la vie (again).

## G77

*The Ecosse Signature was based on which British sports car?*

**B.    AC 3000 ME**

The Ecosse Signature represented the last throw of the dice for the AC 3000ME, a car that was beset by misfortune after misfortune.

Developed from a one-off prototype, the Diablo, created by Peter Bohanna and Robin Stables, the AC 3000 ME was first shown as a non-running prototype at the 1973 Motor Show, where its muscular lines attracted a lot of interest from potential buyers.

AC hoped to have it in production the following year at a price of somewhere between £3400 and £3800, but delay followed delay, and it was 1978 before it finally became available. Rampant inflation and high development costs, partly attributable to the introduction of the Type Approval Regulations, meant that its price had risen to £11,032. And even at that price AC lost money on every car built.

Sales were woefully slow and, worse still, its maker was in financial difficulty. In 1981, however, a light flickered at the end of the tunnel. Ghia, the Ford-owned styling house, showed a rebodied 3000 ME at the Geneva Motor Show, where its spectacular lines caused a sensation. There was some talk of Ford putting it into production but, alas, nothing came of it.

AC decided to cease vehicle production in 1984, but the 3000 ME lived on. Now built under licence by a new company, A C (Scotland) PLC, production moved to Hillington, near Glasgow, and work commenced on an Alfa Romeo V6-powered* mark 2 version. Unfortunately, it was another false dawn, and the project ended in 1985 when A C (Scotland) went into Receivership.

It wasn't quite the end for the 3000ME, however, as Aubrey Woods, who had worked with the BRM and Matra racing teams before joining A C (Scotland) teamed up with a group that included John Parsons, a former Ford development engineer.

With Wood and Parsons now at the helm, the 3000 ME went under a new metamorphosis, this time emerging as the Ecosse Signature. Although based on the ME, the Signature had a restyled body, was powered by a turbocharged 2.0 litre Fiat engine and featured an ingenious self-levelling suspension system.

The Signature was shown at the 1988 Motor Show and was tested by *Performance Car* magazine the following year. Although the Signature was still a work-in-progress, its performance and handling came in for much praise from the magazine. In spite of this, its makers were unable to find the additional funding they required to turn it into a production car. The project was therefore reluctantly abandoned, thus bringing the AC 3000ME's story to a sad conclusion.

*The 3000ME took its name from its mid-engined configuration and the 3.0 litre Ford *Essex* V6 that powered it.

### G78

*For which of these American car manufacturers did John Z. DeLorean **not** work?*

**B.    Ford**

In all the hullabaloo surrounding the car company that that bore his name, it's easy to forget that John Zachary DeLorean was a gifted engineer with, at least until he fell out of favour at General Motors in the early 1970s, a strong track record of success.

Born in 1925, De Lorean graduated from the Lawrence Institute of Technology in 1948, his studies having been interrupted by World War 2. He subsequently attended the Chrysler Institute of Engineering, graduating in 1952 with a master's degree in Automotive Engineering.

De Lorean worked as engineer with Chrysler for a short time before joining Packard, where he was instrumental in improving the company's *Ultramatic* automatic transmission. Following Packard's merger with Studebaker, DeLorean was headhunted by General Motors and joined the company's Pontiac division.

At Pontiac, DeLorean played a significant role in the introduction of the GTO muscle car, a vehicle that did much to enhance the company's image with younger buyers. Consequently, he was promoted to head the Pontiac division, thereby becoming, at 40, the youngest-ever division head in General Motors history.

A further promotion followed in 1969, when he took over the reigns at Chevrolet, General Motors' largest division. His run of success continued at Chevrolet, but his colourful image and maverick ways did not always find favour with General Motors' most senior executives.

In 1973, a year after DeLorean had been appointed Vice President of Car and Truck Production for General Motors, he left the company. The official line was that he had resigned, but there were whispers that he had been forced out.

Whatever the truth of the matter, DeLorean now embarked on a path that would lead him to infamy. He never did work for Ford, but was offered the chance by a group of investors to become the President of American Motors Corporation, taking what would become the DMC-12 with him. However, the opportunity passed him by, and he pressed ahead with plans to manufacture his gull-winged, stainless steel-clad coupé independently.

The rest is, as they say, history.

# G79

*Which company owned Citroën prior to Peugeot's acquisition of it in 1976?*

**D.   Michelin**

Founded in 1919 by André-Gustave Citroën, the fledgling company attracted the interest of General Motors. The two companies entered into discussions and several GM officials crossed the Atlantic to visit the Citroën factory. Ultimately, however, GM decided against purchasing the French manufacturer.

André Citroën thus remained at the helm of the company that bore his name. In the years that followed, he employed modern mass production techniques in his factory, set up a dealer and service network across France and provided signs for the expanding French road network.

By December 1934, however, Citroën's finances were in a perilous state, the principal cause of which was the cost incurred in developing the revolutionary Traction Avant model and building a new factory (in effect, Citroën tore down the old factory and built a new one without stopping production) in which to manufacture it.

Salvation came in the form of Citroën's biggest creditor, Michelin, who took control of the company at the request of the French government. Replaced by Pierre Michelin as the company's Chairman, André Citroën died in 1935.

Michelin continued to hold a majority stake in Citroën for the next four decades. Car production ceased during the second world war and was slow to resume when peace returned to Europe, but the 1950s to the early 1970s would be Citroën's greatest era.

In 1955, it released the groundbreaking DS; in the 1960s, it acquired both Panhard and Maserati and joined forces with NSU to develop and manufacture rotary engines under the aegis of a new company, Comotor; and in the first half of the 1970s it launched the GS and CX models, both of which were voted European Car of the Year.

Heady stuff, but by 1974 Citroën was once again in severe financial peril, a consequence of the failure of the rotary-engined project, the cost of developing new models, the effect of the global energy crisis and, prior to the GS, the lack of a mid-sized car with which to compete in a very lucrative market sector.

And that's where Peugeot stepped in...

## G80

*'Autocar & Motor' advised their readers to sell "your grandmother and the rest of your family, your dog, your cat and anything else to hand" in order to have which car?*

### C. Lotus Elan M100

On the face of it, the Lotus Elan M100 had all the ingredients required in order to succeed: an impeccable pedigree, fresh, modern styling, reliable Isuzu running gear, a properly-funded development programme, strong performance, and superb roadholding.

It was launched to a rapturous reception (*Autocar & Motor* called it "the world's first front-wheel drive supercar" and other commentators were just as effusive about its qualities) and even won a design award. But there was a problem. Two problems, in fact.

The first problem was prejudice. The M100's front-wheel drive configuration, supple ride and ludicrously high levels of adhesion meant that some people (ones who were, perhaps, used to visiting hedges backwards...) were instantly dismissive of it.

And then there was the economy. The M100 came in over budget and consequently went on sale at a higher price than Lotus had envisaged. That might still have been okay, but a global recession followed on the heels of the M100's introduction. As belts were tightened, demand for the M100 fell.

Lotus pulled the plug on the M100 in 1992, only to bring it back as an even more expensive limited edition (of 800 cars) in 1994. And this time it
sold well. Production ended in 1995, after which the tooling was shipped to Korea, where Kia briefly produced their own version of the M100.

# About The Authors

## David M. Milloy (writer)

David practised law for over twenty years before escaping from the legal profession in order to fulfil a childhood ambition by becoming a motoring writer.

Since changing career, David has written for a number of publications in both printed and digital media, including Classic Car Weekly, Absolute Lotus and Influx.

This is David's second book. His first, *The Ultimate Unofficial F1 Quiz Book*, is also available from Amazon. He's currently working on his next book, information about which will be posted on his website:

**www.thelosthighway.online**

## Marcus T. Ward (illustrations)

Living in Staffordshire not too far away from the Cheshire and Shropshire borders, Marcus is a digital artist mostly using the Affinity Designer drawing package.

Whilst recuperating from a back injury in early 2018, he decided to attempt to take up drawing to ease his boredom. He draws in a variety of styles from simple illustrative drawings to near life-like works.

Trained in electronics and software engineering, the only previous drawing experience was CAD work designing printed circuit boards and industrial rechargeable battery packs.

Marcus will admit to being stuck in a time bubble due to his interest and love of 1960's & 1970's rock music and cars.

More of Marcus's work can be seen at – and purchased from - his redbubble store:

**redbubble.com/people/marcustward/shop**